Suffolk Way

Suffolk Way

Ian St.John

First edition 1993
Published by Footpath Guides

SECOND EDITION 1999
Published by: Suffolk Walker
Old Hall
East Bergholt
Suffolk
CO7 6TG

Printed by St.Edmundsbury Press
Bury St.Edmunds IP33 3TU

ISBN 0 9520880 1 0

COVER Detail from *Autumnal Sunset* an oil sketch painted by John Constable RA. People are walking the East Bergholt to Stratford St.Mary public footpath nearly 200 years ago during the autumn of 1812. Suffolk Way takes you along this ancient footpath (page 12).
CourtesyofV&APictureLibrary

Suffolk Way

Ian St.John

Second Edition

Suffolk Walker

CONTENTS

THANKS

My thanks are extended to those people who have written to me asking for a copy of Suffolk Way. It had become out of print and the requests helped me put aside other writing and concentrate on this new fully revised edition.

Several people have given me honest comments on the route of the first version of the Suffolk Way. I am especially grateful to the walking partners Ray Cook and John Last, and to Alan Tong but also to Stephanie Hammond, Derek Keeble and J.E.B. Smith. The route has changed for the better, giving more country paths, fewer country roads, and the improved walk eliminates short lengths of double backing.

Thanks also to Dr.Colin Pendleton, member of the Conservation team, Archaeological Service, Suffolk County Council, for welcoming me and making room in his office for me to conduct my search through the parish files of registered archaeological sites.

My natural history research was greatly aided by reference to literature on National Nature Reserves, Sites of Special Scientific Interest, and County Wildlife Sites made available to me by Sue Holden from the Suffolk Team, English Nature; Dorothy Casey, Wildlife Sites Advisor, Suffolk Wildlife Trust; Sue Hooton, County Ecologist with Suffolk County Council and Celia Richardson, Project Officer of the Dedham Vale and Stour Valley Countryside Project, Suffolk County Council. Thank you.

And last, but by no means least, special thanks to everyone in Old Hall Computer Consultancy.

DEDICATION

For my son Rowan

INTRODUCTION

Suffolk Way is a 109 mile (174 km) walk offering the essential character of rural Suffolk. It starts at Flatford, a hamlet associated with the English landscape painter John Constable, whose paintings of the surrounding countryside epitemise the beauty and tranquility to be found here. The way takes you through Constable Country northwest via Box Valley in the Dedham Vale Area of Outstanding Natural Beauty to the beautiful medieval wool town of Lavenham with its remarkable concentration of ancient timber-framed houses.

As a " High Plains drifter" (without the horse) you head northeast through traditional Suffolk villages and across miles of open wheat and beet boulder clay country coming to experience and appreciate why locally the area is known as High Suffolk. Approaching Halesworth the soil lightens as you enter the coastal landscape called the Sandlings and hence east through pasture and marsh beside the River Blyth to the sea at Walberswick. It is here that you turn north along Suffolk's Heritage Coast to finish in Lowestoft.

Your walk will take you down public footpaths and bridleways that should be reasonably convenient to pass along. If you find to your delight the paths are unobstructed by hedges, cross-field paths are clear of crops, field-edge paths are not ploughed out, ground cover on them has been cut, and deep ditches across your path are spanned with bridges, please write and thank the County Highways Authority who have a duty to protect and maintain Suffolk Way. Also let them known about any problems you may have encountered. Their address is:

Countryside Service, Environment and Transport Dept., Suffolk County Council, St. Edmunds House, County Hall, Ipswich, Suffolk IP4 1LZ I. Tel: 01473 230000

TRANSPORT

Phone Suffolk County Council TravelLine 0645583358 for help. Monday to Friday 8.15am to 5.45pm and Saturday 8.30am to 4pm.

TRAIN I recommend you use the train to Manningtree station and walk the three miles across grazing marshes to the beginning of the Suffolk Way at Flatford. Manningtree is a main line station on the London Liverpool Street to Norwich line. This walk is shown on a map on page 10 and described on page 11. At the end of your walk you enter Lowestoft. This Suffolk seaside town has two branch lines, one with trains to Ipswich and hence to London, and the other to Norwich.
For National Rail Enquiries telephone 0345 48 49 50.
Railtrack passenger timetable website is
http://www.railtrack.co.uk

COACH There are National Express coaches that travel between Colchester in Essex along the A12 to Ipswich in Suffolk. You can ask to be dropped off at the " Four Sisters" midway along the route which is on the outskirts of East Bergholt. From here you walk through the village to Flatford. National Express Enquiries 0990 808080

BUS Use local Eastern Counties buses to East Bergholt. Phone 01473 253734 for information.

CAR Please do not go to the start of the walk by car. Flatford is a honeypot site for tourists who travel by car looking at the place the English landscape painter John Constable made famous. Use the train, coach, bus, bicycle or walk.

ACCOMMODATION

Information about where to spent the night after a good day walking is available from tourist information centres. The main one for Suffolk all year round is in Sudbury 01787 881320

Other tourist information centres are: Flatford 01206 299460 Easter to October. Lavenham 01787 248207 Easter to October. Ipswich 01473 258070. Southwold 01502 724729. Lowestoft 01502 523000

MAPS

The best and most up-to-date maps for walking the Suffolk Way are ordnance survey Explorer Maps and The Broads Outdoor Leisure Map. These show field boundaries and other landmarks not shown on the Landranger maps or the guide book..

The Explorer maps you need are numbers:
197, 196, 211, 212, 230, 231 and Outdoor Leisure Map 40

Pathfinder map numbers for Suffolk Way are:
925, 946, 965, 966, 986, 1006, 1007, 1008, 1029, 1030, 1052, 1053. It may be possible to use this guide book to find the route without reference to maps, but I do not advise it. At the very least use ordnance survey Landranger Maps 134, 155, 156 and 169.

The Landranger map number, followed by Pathfinder map numbers, are shown in brackets in this book to the right of the Explorer number above the maps.

It may sound daft but do not forget your **compass**. There may be occasions when you lose your sense of direction.

The walk in from
MANNINGTREE STATION to FLATFORD

3 kilometres / **2 miles**   **Map 197** (169 & 155 / 1053)

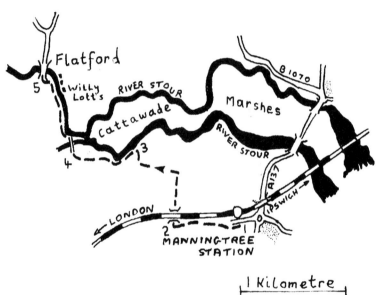

1 Leave the station entrance turning half right to walk down the slope to the lower car park. Turn left across the tarmac to the verge and walk across the short path over rough grass to a track. Turn right along the farm track parallel with the railway.

10

MANNINGTREE STATION to FLATFORD

2 Turn right under the railway bridge. Continue along a grass track until you reach the river. I hope you have a pair of binoculars with you

Cattawade Marshes *is a 218 acre (82ha.) area of undisturbed neutral grassland grazed by cattle that is designated a Site of Special Scientific Interest by English Nature.*

Bounded by the southern tidal channel and northern freshwater channels of the River Stour there are marshy pools and dykes with riverside and fenland vegetation providing cover for nesting Shoveler, Teal, Tufted Duck and Water Rail.

The old grazing marsh is mainly couch grass, perennial rye-grass and Yorkshire fog. pushed up in places by ant-hills. A haven for breeding Waders and wildfowl such as Lapwing., Oystercatcher and Redshank, Ringed Plover and Shelduck.

3 Turn left along the tidal defence bank to the concrete tidal barrier.

4 Walk across the concrete barrier above sluice gates and then along the tow path .

Willy Lott's House *Over the River Stour to your right you get a view of the house that featured in the English landscape painter John Constable's most famous work "The Haywain". Just past the house is Flatford Mill owned at one time by Constable's father now by the National Trust and occupied by the Field Studies Council.*

5 Arrive at the bridge over the River Stour. The start of your walk along Suffolk Way.

FLATFORD -- STRATFORD ST.MARY

4 km / **2.5 miles**   **Map 197** (169 & 155 / 1053)

1 Leave Flatford Bridge on the opposite side to Bridge Cottage over the stile by the metal access contraption towards Dedham. Follow left bank of Stour past pollard willows to Fen Bridge.

FLATFORD -- STRATFORD ST.MARY

2 Cross the footbridge and go up the path then hoggin track called Fen Lane. Cross Dead River Bridge. At the bend climb over the metal stile ahead of you in the hedge. Proceed half-right uphill across pasture to the top *(View over Dedham Vale, also known as Constable Country)* over a metal stile to Flatford Lane.

3 Cross the lane, up the steps onto footpath before stile. Turn left along this path next to the lane.

4 *Come out onto the lane near the top of Fen Lane (seen in Constable's "Dedham Vale:Morning" etc.). Walk Flatford Lane to the church in East Bergholt.*

Church of St.Mary the Virgin. *Perpendicular style. Flint, brick and stone. Tower begun in 1525 but not finished. Dinky cupola added in 18th century. Sun-dial above porch "Time passeth away like a shadow". Unique bellcage round back of church. Built possibly 1541. Peg-tiled pyramid louvered roof above oak lattice and boarded sides. Inverted Bells rung by pushing the shoulder stocks.*

5 Leave the churchyard through the gate with lamp above it and walk into village. Cross the street and go down the lane beside the Post Office (unmarked Cemetery Lane).
Where the lane descends *(scene of Constable's "Autumnal Sunset," a detail of which is on the cover of this book)* veer left down a footpath *(depicted on the painting).*
Over the footbridge, then the drift, and diagonally up the cross-field path. Walk the field-edge to where Dead Lane *(Green Lane)* cuts across the path. Cross Dead Lane and walk the track ahead towards Stratford St.Mary Church. Where the track bends to the left continue straight on over a cross field path to the B 1029 , Then left and right to the church.

13

STRATFORD ST.MARY -- HIGHAM

2.5 km / **1.5 miles** (Total 6.5 km / 4 ml**) Map 196** (155 / 1053)

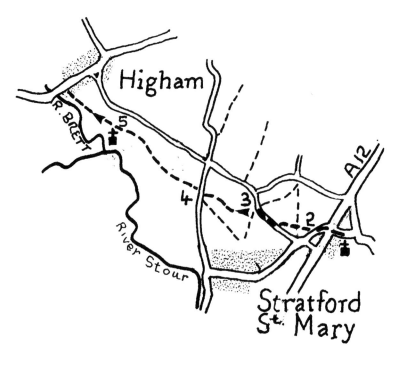

Stratford St.Mary *An important Roman road crossed the River Stour at a ford here. The village was bypassed in 1975 by the busy A12 Colchester - Ipswich road which runs approximately on the original line of the Roman road. A bassoon used to hang in the south aisle in St.Marys Church but was stolen some time ago. I guess there will be one less musician in heaven*

14

STRATFORD ST.MARY -- HIGHAM

1 Cross road opposite the church. Walk down under the A12 bridge. About 40 metres before the junction turn right climbing the grass bank. Over the railing. Cross the narrow field end to the wall corner.

2 Continue on behind the garden and near the old school house onto School Lane. Turn right up School Lane for about 100 metres.

3 Turn left over the stile and walk the right edge to another stile. Over this and cross the small field besde the hawthorn hedge. Over the stile and across to behind the tennis court. Climb the railing, pass behind the court and in the right hand corner go between the fence and hedge. Tend left round Yew Tree House garden to cross a stile. Turn right onto Higham Road to opposite Yew Tree House..

4 Turn left on the field-edge track then path that skirts a shelter belt. *Photographed from the air the area each side of Higham Road shows a complex remnant field system of rectangular and circular enclosures and ring ditches of unknown age.*
Quite soon the right of way leaves the field edge and veers right crossing the arable field to about twenty metres right of the brick farm building, passing through the mixed shelter belt. Cross the farm track to the stile in the corner of the paddock. Over the stile follow the left fence over the next stile onto Higham Hall drive. Higham Church is to your right. *Higham Church and Hall are isolated from the main village next to the confluence of the River Brett with the River Stour.*

5 Through the metal kissing gate cross the field. (The river to your left is the Brett). Over the stile, under the chestnut tree and left of the fence to another stile. Over this and down a tunnel-like path out into Higham

HIGHAM -- WITHERMARSH GREEN

4 km / 2.5 miles (Total 10.5 km / 6.5 ml) **Map 196** (155/1053)

HIGHAM -- WITHERMARSH GREEN

1 Left to Higham Bridge over the River Brett *(view of Higham Church)*. Just past "The Bauble" after the corner turn left along the field-edge path. Right at the field corner and about half way along this large field take a short left to a corner. pass through the hedge by the poplar tree.

2 Cross the grassy track and walk straight on along the field edge. Over the stile to the left of the low brick wall *(remains of Lower Barn)*. Follow the field edge ahead. Over the stile and cross the rough grass to the ford and footbridge *(tributary of the Stour)*.

3 The way is not over the bridge, instead turn right along Langham Mill Lane *(track)*. Walk the right bend then soon after take the left bend and walk to the road..
This staggered crossroad of the tarmac B1068 with Langham Mill Lane and Snow Hill Lane was an important site possibly of burial mounds because aerial photos show cropmarks of a group of five ring ditches on the left of Langham Mill Lane here with others nearby on either side of Snow Hill Lane.

4 Turn left a short way and then right along Snow Hill Lane. *The upper part of this green lane, with its pretty name, gives clear signs of its antiquity- its sunken profile showing centuries of wear by cart, horse and people; the lane hedge banks; coppiced and pollarded oak; the wonderful variety of woody species in the lane hedges- English elm, holly, sloe, elder, maple, spindle and hawthorn among others. To top it all there is the splendid view over the Brett Valley and another to Higham Church..* Pass the turn off to Eastfields Farm.

5 Suffolk Way does not take you all the way to Withermarsh Green, instead, turn left up the drive passing on the right of Bobwrights Farmhouse and barn. Turn right along a high track between fields. Continue along the track to Hudsons Lane.

WITHERMARSH GREEN -- POLSTEAD

5.5km/ **3.5 miles** (Total 16km/10ml) **Map 196** (155/1053 1052)

1 Turn right a few metres then cross the lane continuing left on a field-edge track. Cross Londs Lane hoggin bridleway continuing on the footpath beside the hedge. *(View of Stoke-by-Nayland church ahead).* Leave by the far corner through a sweet chestnut plantation and small wood. Climb the stile by the oak and turn right downhill (with " Rams Farm" down to your right). Right onto the farm drive turn immediately left down the drive to cross the wooden bridge over the River Box at Valley Farm.

2 Follow the track round to the right, continue straight on at the left bend. Over the stile by the metal field gate. Walk the field edge with a hedge to your left to the stile. Over this with the hedge to your right on field-edge path. On the bend head across the field to the corner of an adjacent field. Tend right through poplar plantation onto the field-edge path. At the corner turn left to continue on the field-edge path.

18

WITHERMARSH GREEN -- POLSTEAD

Cropmarks in the large field to your left show a series of linear ditches outlining a field system laid out possibly at only one time. These traces of past farming practice are only visible from the air. What is available to you are the old ash coppice on the hedge bank on your right that may be part of the original field system. At the B1068 right into Stoke-by-Nayland (" Stoke ")

3 Turn left down Church Street to the Church of St.Mary.
Church of St.Mary This large fifteenth century church is situated in the centre of the village. The ornate 120ft. west tower of flint and peach-coloured stone can be seen for miles around. On the far side of the churchyard to the left of the lynch gate is a small building covering a well, down which a servant of Lord Windsor fell to his death in 1603. And in the right hand corner of the churchyard the small brick and slate building was the village lock-up. In School Street are the beautiful sixteenth century former Guildhall and Maltings converted to cottages. Back down Church Street cross the street.Walk down Scotland Street descending into the Box Valley Pass Scotland Place and over the River Box.

4 Left opposite Scotland House over a sleepers and stile. Cross the meadow.Walk with the garden fence on right to stile. Over this and sleeper bridge. Cross meadow and the stile in corner of wood railing. Across sleepers into ornamental garden and follow round to the left across lawn to stile. Climb it and walk through the wood along a broad path over a stile and right along the track to the three-way signpost before the lane.

5 Left with wire fence on your left. Over stile in corner of field. Tend right along tarmac track but turn immediately left along a wide grassy path. Over stile into wood. Veer right across field on the crest. Down the slope, over the stile to the road at Bell's Corner. Cross the road coming in from your right and walk past a garden. Turn right along a footpath to Polstead Green.

POLSTEAD -- BOXFORD

6km/ **4 miles** (Total 22 km / 14 ml) **Map 196** (155 /1052,1029)

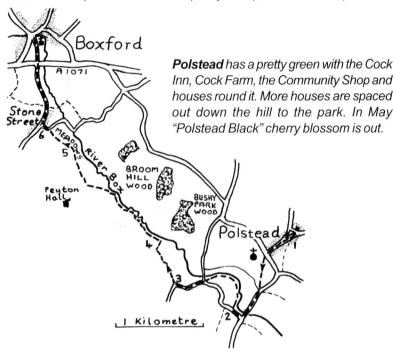

Polstead has a pretty green with the Cock Inn, Cock Farm, the Community Shop and houses round it. More houses are spaced out down the hill to the park. In May "Polstead Black" cherry blossom is out.

1 Down the hill. Cross the road and through the metal kissing gate into Polstead Park. Cross the park aiming to the right of the white Park Lodge through a kissing gate. Turn right on the road then right along Mill Lane and pass the old Watermill.

2 Right, ocross a water meadow. Over a stile, through a willow plantation*(see the church spire)*. 0nto ield-edge path, and kissing gate onto the lane. *(Down the track to your right is a ford and footbridge over the Box)*. Straight up this to the left bend.

3 Turn right and tend left along the edge of a field but about half way along weave through a small wood to a kissing gate. Walk across meadows through kissing gates and over sleeper bridges with the River Box right. As you approach the ugly overhead transmission towers look over to your right to the two woods on the valley side.

20

Bushy Park Wood.*on the right has a fascinating mixture of medieval and post-medieval features. A sinuous west boundary bank and double bank on part of the south edge. Two natural flushes within the wood give rise to streams that flow through the wood to join the Box. The canopy is mainly alder and ash in the central area with a struggling understorey of hazel coppice. Beneath this, yellow archangel, wood melick and wood millet provide strong botanical evidence that this woodland is ancient.*

Broom Hill Wood *on the left is another ancient wood. Ash, maple, oak, with hazel coppice and regenerating wild cherry and holly,has been invaded by sycamore and a hand-planted acre of poplars. Under all these species can be found dogs mercury, bluebells, primroses and wood anemone.*

4 Continue across the meadows. At the wet corner and hedge turn left. In the corner go through the kissing gate and turn right along the hoggin track which changes to tarmac.

5 To your right are two low-lying wet fields.

River box Meadows *The first, and largest, you pass by is bordered on the east by the River Box lined with mature willow next to which is a waterlogged area dominated with fen vegetation such as sedges with rushes and meadowsweet, and less common plants such as purple loosestrife and square-stalked St.Johns-wort This fen extends north-west into the smaller meadow with. plant species like ragged robin and water forget-me-not. There is some rough grazing outside the fen areas. If you are lucky you may see hobby, barn owl or green sandpiper.*

6 Turn left on the lane to the junction. Turn right through Stone Street At the A1071 cross over and walk down the road into Boxford.

BOXFORD -- GROTON WOOD

5 km / **3 miles** (Total 27 km / 17 ml) **Map 196** (155 / 1029)

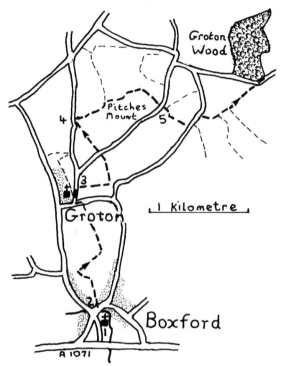

Church of St.Mary *south porch is a strange pale confection of Caen stone. On the north side the fourteenth century (or earlier) porch is possibly the oldest in England.*

1 Walk round to the right along the main street

*The open double-arched small building on your right looks like a bus shelter that's because it is a bus shelter. Before that it was a fire station. Notice the initials BG, originally it was **B**oxford **G**aol.* Continue to the White Hart. *Early in the 20th century the dare-devil adventurer Tornado Smith operated a Wall of Death from the Inn. He also had a lion which he exercised through the village and is thought to be buried under the Inn forecourt*

22

BOXFORD -- GROTON WOOD

2 Opposite the White Hart cross the street and go up the track.
Pass the Bowls club uphill to the playing field, keeping to the left edge,
pass the brick pavilion and adventure playground into the field *(view of
Groton Church)*. Turn right by field-edge path to the corner and left on
the grass path across the field to a track. follow this to the lane to the
right of the Dutch barn. Left to junction. *(Keep straight on for the Fox and
Hounds)* and turn right passing Groton Church .
3 Turn right along a path beside a ditch. In the corner turn left. Walk
edge of field with wood on right. Cross lane by house and go on path
across field to a lane layby. Turn right and at end of layby turn right along
sunken footpath.
4 Pass old wooden double gates. Up steps and cross rough meadow
over stile and diagonally cross lawn to stile and enter wood. Walk to the
left about quarter round the curious Pitches Mount.**Pitches Mount** *is a
medieval ring motte on high ground in Groton Park. There are traces of a
fosse (ditch) surrounding the mount which is almost 200ft diameter rising
to 20ft with a banked rim.* Out to the field, right to walk the outside edge
of wood that invaded Pitches Mount. At the end of the wood tend right
to the field corner. Walk field-edge path with hedge on left. Cross sleeper
bridge in corner. Walk half-right across field to the corner by the three-
way sign. Cross sleeper bridge. Follow right side of ditch to lane.
5 Cross over and follow path on right of ditch. In the corner tend left
over the ditch and then right to walk the left side of the hedge. After
about 40 metres go up the bank through a hedge gap. From the field
corner turn left on the right-hand side of the hedge. Cross the sleepers
onto the lane by Hayes House. Turn left and at Poplars Farm turn right
through the farmyard. Turn left between two oaks to the arable field corner.
Keep on the right of the hedge to the corner. Over the sleepers and walk
on the right of the ditch. Over an earth bridge then along the next field
edge coming out onto the lane by a house opposite Groton Wood.

GROTON WOOD -- KERSEY

5km/ **3 miles**(Total 32 km / 20 ml)**Map 196** (155 /1029,1030)

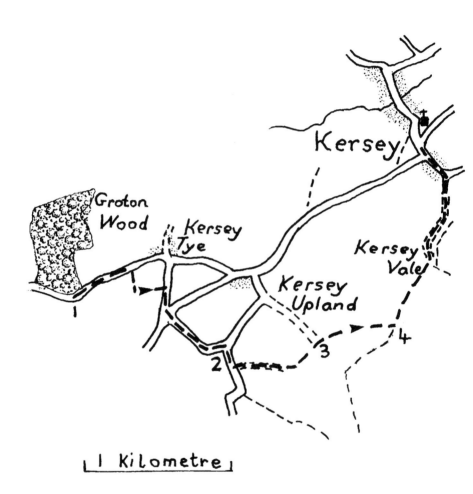

1 Kilometre

GROTON WOOD -- KERSEY

Groton Wood. As you enter there are tall wild cherry trees to your right. There are groups of Cherry dotted over the southern two-thirds of the wood. Being a plant that colonises relatively young woodland it comes as no surprise that the lower two-thirds was at one time fields. The area is cross-crossed with remnant field banks, ditches and stock ponds preserved by the wood. The wood was probably planted gradually in the 16th and 17th centuries by Winthrop Estate workers. The northern third of is dominated by the largest stand of small-leaved lime coppice in Suffolk. This tree was dominant across most of High Suffolk before the Neolithic clearances and has survived here, a living link with the primeval Suffolk Wildwood. The south boundary of this ancient part has a tremendous sinuous double woodbank. The north boundary by contrast is straight. To the north of this boundary an area equivalent to the present ancient part to the south of the boundary was grubbed out

1 Walk back down the lane past the house and by the oak, Right over the wide earth bridge to cross the field to a point between the cross field telegraph poles. Left following the line of the poles to the lane. Right and at the crossroads go straight over on the By Road. Bringing you to William's Green junction.

2 Right and, past Old Mill House, left on track. Part way along the small plantation to your left, veer left through it *(note the small-leaved lime in the hedge)* onto field-edge to the track.

3 Turn right and immediately curve left on the track *(glimpse of Kersey Church)* which moves from right of the hedge to the left. Under oak in corner leave Kersey Upland and go straight across the arable field to the signpost down in Kersey Vale.

4 Turn left beside the ditch. Near the corner cross the sleepers and through the right edge of the wood. Then round Vale Cottage to the left, onto the drive and walk towards the church . At the junction turn left downhill past Kersey church

25

KERSEY -- ROSE GREEN

4 km/ **2.5 miles**(Total 36km/22.5ml)**Map 196** (155/1030,1029)

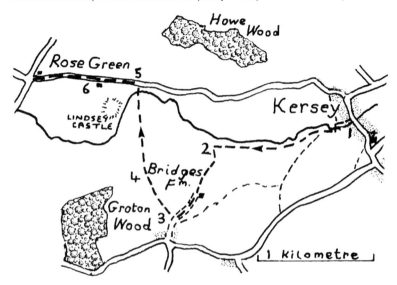

Kersey is a small, compact, very pretty, Suffolk village.. Kersey gave its name to cloth first produced in the parish. There are cottages in the village with long lattice-paned first floor windows that gave plenty of light to the weavers in the Middle Ages. The splash at the bottom is a tributary of the Brett.

1 Descend into the secluded vale down the main street. After the splash turn left down a track. *(On the corner is 17th century "Kedges End" at one time a wool merchant's house and later owned by a horse doctor. There is horse tail dangling from the eave.).* Go over the footbridge and turn left to go over another footbridge. Climb the steps to the field. BEWARE OF ELECTRIFIED FENCE. Turn right to the end of the field . Walk on the grass track to the corner, then left to a narrow metal gate by telegraph pole posts.**2** Through gate walking to the left of the hedge to the galvanised field gate. *(From near the ramshackle barn view Kersey church)* turn left up the farm track and veer right along it to Bridges Farm. Go through the farmyard *(rosettes on the barn wall)* and down the farm drive to the end of the right-hand edge.

26

3 Turn right at the signpost and cross the large arable field. You have the right of way. Walk straight out. Do not be tempted to walk to the hedge over to your left *(beyond which you can see Groton Wood).* Instead, after a while, tend to the right to reach a point just to the left of the hedge coming in from your right. You are still in the middle of the big field!

4 Continue through the middle tending right and keeping away from the hedge on your left that will turn away from you. Walk over to the oak in the hedge and sleepers (Phew!). Cross the smaller field to the poplar trees.by the yellow marker post. Cross the sleepers to walk a wooded path to the lane with a view of Howe Wood to your right.

5 Left and just past the lane joining on your right, look to the left across the field. The low wooded area hides Lindsey Castle.

__Lindsey Castle__ is a Norman defensive earthwork first mentioned in the twelfth century as held by Adam de Cockfield, It is a Motte and Bailey castle. There is a large earthen mound covering about half an acre (the motte) which in this case is low, being only 3.6 m high, on top of which would have stood a timber tower. This is surrounded by a 4.5 acre enclosure (the bailey) with a massive internal boundary bank (2.5m high), on top of which would have been a timber palisade, and outside of this is a massive ditch (2.7m deep). Continue to walk along the lane to St.James Chapel. *__St.James Chapel__ was built early in the thirteenth century of flint and stone. The south wall with two different sized lancet windows and doorway are original. There is a late 13th cent. piscina (stone basin in niche for washing communion vessels) with pointed trefoiled arch. West end has a bricked up window and early Tudor brick doorway. North wall one window was bricked up and plastered, the other converted into a doorway. East end has the remains of a three light window.. Early use was by monks of St.Edmunds associated with Lindsey Castle. Later centuries saw the chapel survive intact as a stable and calf pen.*

6 Down the lane to White Rose Inn,

ROSE GREEN -- BRENT ELEIGH

5.5km/ **3.5 miles** (Total 41.5km / 26ml) **Map 196** (155 /1029)

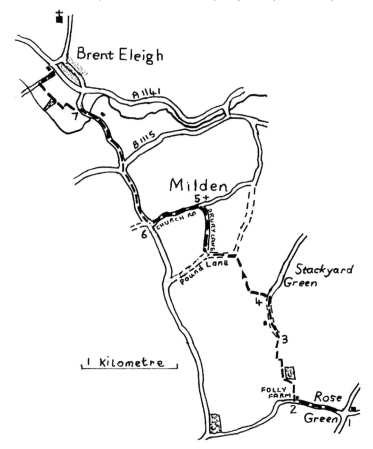

1 After pub go over crossroad. Walk lane to the far side of Folly Farm.

2 Turn right to follow the field-edge footpath. A bit before the wood turn diagonally left to cut off the field corner Walk beside the wood and continue on the same line to a solitary oak. Turn left to a ditch. Now turn right beside the ditch crossing to the clump of willow surrounding the small pond and onto the bridleway.

ROSE GREEN -- BRENT ELEIGH

3 Turn left along the bridleway passing through Spring Farm House garden onto the drive. Go down the drive a short way.

4 Turn left on the bridleway. Tend left beside the ditch then between two hedges. Turn right to Serens Hall. Head north opposite the Hall along tarmac Drury Lane

Moat You are walking through the parish of Milden. Before the junction with Church Road look through the hedge to your right . Just beyond the hedge you see the remains of a moat. It is the west dry arm two metre deep. Another short section is on the corner. The moat is occupied by the eighteenth century rectory.
View At the junction take in the view.
Milden To your right is Milden Church. There is a theory that Milden got its name during the 5th to 7th centuries from settlers called Meldinga who lived round here. Part of their diet was the abundant edible weed Fat hen or Melde Chenopodum album.
Trig Pillar In the far corner of the playing field opposite the church spot the trig.pillar.

5 Walk back down Church Road to the junction with Powney Road.
Village Sign near the telephone is a unique painted metal sculpture of Melde.
6 Turn right along the road. Go over the crossroad with the B1115 and descend towards Brent Eleigh.

7 A couple of hundred metres before the junction turn left on footpath between hedge and fence. Follow field-edge path round to left uphill and turn right at outer corner Continue on field-edge path beside old hedge to end of green lane . *View of hall across valley.* Continue and cross field turning right down Cock lane to the pub.

BRENT ELEIGH -- LAVENHAM

4km / **2.5 miles** (Total 45.5km/28.5ml) **Map 196** (155 / 1029)

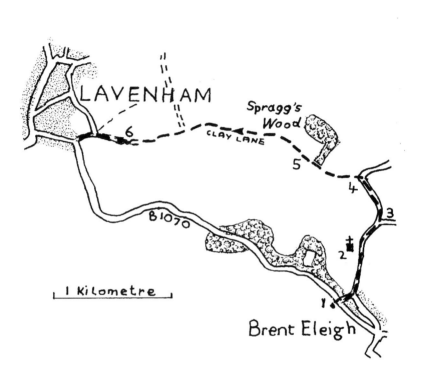

1 Cross the road and along Hall Road into the village, . At the junction stay on Hall Road cross the Brett over the bridge to about half way up the hill.
Continue up the hill to the church on the edge of the settlement.

St.Mary's Church. Enter by the carved fourteenth century South door. Inside is a fine example of Jacobean (Period of James 1 of England, 1603-25) pulpit and box pews. On the walls are the remnants of unique medieval paintings.

30

3 Continue up the hill passing the turn off. Over to your right is Langley Wood a five hectare woodland designated by English Nature a Site of Special Scientific Interest.

Langley Wood is on the site of an ancient wood with oak and ash standards. Along the lane you can see a pollard oak on the wood edge. There is evidence of yew and oak planting. Langley Wood has an understory dominated by hazel. Ia addition there are some elm, small-leaved lime, birch, holly, wild cherry and maple. Among the bramble and dog's mercury are ancient woodland indicator species such as nettle-leaved bellflower and wood sorrel. The wood also contains a stream and two ponds where many species enjoy the damp conditions including Male Fern and Buckler Fern.

4 At the right hand bend turn off left along the remarkable ancient way called Clay Lane.

Clay Lane You appear to pass into a wood. In point of fact you are walking a wooded lane adjacent to the southwest boundary of an ancient wood. Look to your right and you can see you are outside the massive medieval boundary bank of the wood.

Spragg's Wood is a five hectare ancient wood that has been designated a SSSI. The wood consists of oak-ash-hazel standards with an understorey of hazel coppice. Within this coppice is willow, wood and hedge hawthorn and remarkably the rare wild pear. On the ground grows dog's mercury with plentiful primrose and a sprinkling of the common spotted orchid among many other species.

5 Continue on the ancient green lane called.*Clay Lane with drainage ditches each side of the central lane and old coppice stools on the boundary banks.*

6 Pass Clayhill Farm. Walk down the drive to the junction with a lane. Turn left, and at the junction with Brent Eleigh Road turn right. Go up the road to Lavenham.

LAVENHAM -- PRESTON ST.MARY

4km/ **2.5mls** (49.5km/31ml) **Maps196&211** (155/1029, 1006)

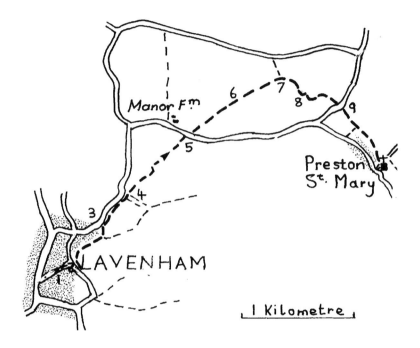

1 Find the market place. Walk down Prentice Street between Angel Hotel and Great House Restaurant with *lovely view of the fields*. At the bottom cross the lane to walk over a brick footbridge under which flows a tributary of the Brett.

2 Along the path left to the field. Cross the field over the rise where you see the telegraph pole beside the wooded stream dell ahead. Follow the field-edge path round the wood to a track and turn left.

3 Before the concrete bridge turn right along the edge of the field with the stream and then minor road to your left. Turn the corner for 20 metres and descend the steps.

32

LAVENHAM -- PRESTON ST.MARY

4 Cross track and walk beside left bank of stream (ditch)/hedge. Walk the field-edge path to corner. Go through gap onto the lane.

5 Turn right and shortly turn left off the lane on a grass track beside a hedge. Cross a wide earth bridge over a stream. Follow the field indentation round to your right. After a further 50m or so pass through a gap in the hedge through a group of conifers.

6 Follow the line of telegraph poles to the left of the hedge.

7 At the wide gap turn right on the grass track with a hedge on your left. At the corner follow round to the right Pass through the gap over the earth bridge with concrete edges.

8 Go along the grassy track following the leftward bend of the wide hedge. At the end of the bend turn right over an earth bridge and narrow gap in the hedge into a field corner. Walk beside the hedge past the house.

Windmill site *Over the other side of the hedge there was once a working windmill.. At 80 metres about sea level this a high place hereabouts. Add to the height a five story brick tower and build on a domecap, fantail and four patent sails. There was enough wind power in 1846 to grind corn between three pairs of stones. About 1919 it stopped and nine years later the mill was demolished. All that remains are the foundations.*

9 Cross the lane and walk beside the hedge towards the church tower. *Great view to your left* . At the corner cross the ditch by earth bridge. Head across the field to the right of the church tower to the outward corner of the hedge opposite. Follow the field-edge path coming out opposite the church on Church Lane and visit the churchyard.

PRESTON ST.MARY -- KETTLEBASTON

2.5km/ **1.5 miles** (Total 52km / 32.5 ml) **Map 211** (155/1006)

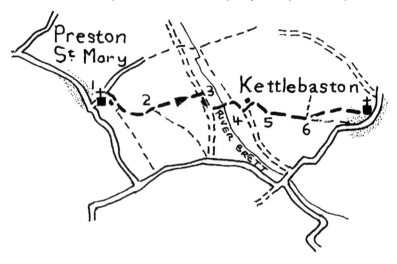

Preston was renamed Preston St.Mary in 1957. The Six Bells pub is up the road. The medieval church of St.Mary is in the centre of the parish though on the far east edge of the settlement near Preston Hall. The **churchyard** is also medieval and although dug up from time to time is a haven for wildlife recognised as such by English Nature and with management advise given by Suffolk Wildlife Trust. A notice inside the gate under the Yew reads:

*"**Wildlife Sanctuary** This churchyard is a sanctuary for wildlife. Many of the plants that flourish here are now rare in Suffolk. For insects, birds and small mammals this is a haven. Because of changes in our countryside, areas like this are valuable and should be cherished. For this reason the churchyard is managed in a way that benefits wildlife. You will find areas left unmown until the plants have seeded and provided food and shelter for the insects and birds that depend on them. The grass is cut and raked off into piles which in themselves form important sheltering places for many creatures."*

PRESTON ST.MARY -- KETTLEBASTON

1 Walk back along Church Lane to field behind churchyard. Right to follow field-edge .Pass Preston Hall *(Remember Preston St.Mary was called Preston). View across upper Brett Valley.*

2 At end of hedge cross the ditch to continue in the same direction on the right of the ditch downhill.

3 On the track turn right. After 100 plus metres look left over the field. Next to the willow is a footbridge. Cross the field and footbridge over the River Brett entering the parish of Kettlebaston, and continue by crossing the pasture and over the stile before a ruined barn.

4 Right through a narrow strip of woodland onto Old Rectory drive. After about 30 metres left up steps into a field. Follow the field-edge path uphill to your left. At the corner turn right uphill across the narrowest part of the field to the outward corner.

5 Cross into the adjacent field and walk the field-edge path with the hedge to your left. Just before the corner turn left over the ditch and hedge turning left down the paddock edge.

6 Cross footbridge. Walk half left across the pasture to a grass track. Go along the track towards the barn. Pass this on the left and cross the farmyard track passing to the left of the barn ruin.

Kettlebaston Hall Moat. *Just past the tumbling barn take a peek through the hedge on your left. You can see the southwest arm of a moat with water in it. This 100 metre by 90 metre moat also has a surviving north-west arm. Other arms are damaged by landscape gardening, the hall drive, and an enlargement into a duck pond.*

7 Cross the paddock towards the church. Go through the churchyard of the Church of St.Mary and yew tunnel onto the lane.

KETTLEBASTON -- BILDESTON

4km/ **2.5miles**(Total56km/35ml)**Maps211&196**(155/1006,1029)

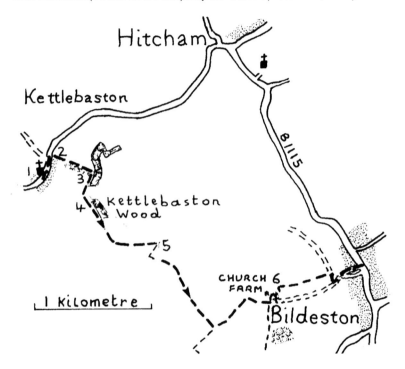

Kettlebaston *is a very small village centred on the church and hall. In 1971 the population was 70. First parish council election was in 1975, and the population declined to 63 by 1981.*

1 Turn left along the lane, through the village, and turn right to climb steps in the field corner next to the bungalow garden.

2 At the corner of the garden walk straight out into the field to cut off the corner. Continue down the line of the wide wooded hedge to the bottom corner of the field.

3 Turn right over the footbridge then left into the corner of the field. Walk beside the wood on your left then to the right of the ditch. Follow this round to the left to the field corner.

4 Cross footbridge and field-edge path next to Kettlebaston Wood.

Kettlebaston Wood is a one hectare ancient wood, and being only half the minimum size required to be recorded in English Nature's Inventory of Ancient Woodland has not been recorded by them. It is a County Wildlife Site. This remnant wood has hornbeam and maple coppice with dead elm. Carpeted with dog's mercury, the woodland floor also has species indicative of ancient woodland such as wood anemone and wood millet.

Remain beside the hedge, over a shallow ditch, field edge again, then a footbridge. Go uphill next to a stream to the corner.

5 Cross the footbridge into Chelsworth parish.Turn right on the field-edge path turning the left-hand corner. Then over the footbridge to the corner. There is a sleeper footbridge to your right but turn left to walk to the left of the hedge. *You can see the cross on the Church of St.Mary.* Come out on the track before the church. Follow the track round to the right,skirting a pond, to the church.

Church of St.Mary occupies high ground, separate from the compact village of Bildeston to the east in the valley. This medieval church is all that remains of the deserted medieval village of Bildeston. The original site of Bildeston Hall with its circular moat were filled in and ploughed over in 1974. Possible hollow ways serving the medieval village suffered a similar fate the previous year. The medieval manorial wood "Bildeston Hall Wood" has survived, and can be seen to the south.

Bildeston Hall Wood is an ancient wood enclosed by a deep ditch and distinct woodbank. Composed mainly of oak, ash and maple there are patches of elm.

Walk back along the track a few metres to before the barn. Turn right between the barn and churchyard across a nettle patch.

6 Turn right on the track and at the next field follow it round to the left to the corner of the plantation. Turn right and walk to the right of the hedge into the valley. At Consent Lane turn right to the junction and left along Church Lane. Take either of the two streets into Bildeston.

BILDESTON -- NAUGHTON

4km/ **2.5 miles** (Total 60km/37.5ml) **Map 196** (155/1029,1030)

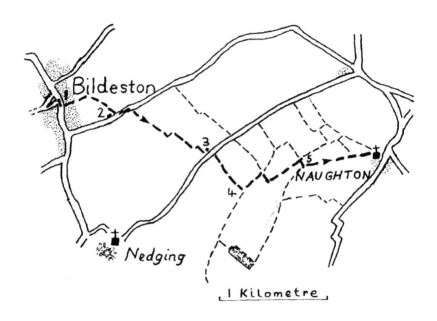

Bildesdon is a large compact village with as its centrepiece a clocktower (1864) that escaped demolition in 1987 after the bell fell during strong winds. This tower stands in the market place. There is a theory that when this market on the Hadleigh-Stowmarket road prospered the people deserted the village sited on the hill near the church and moved round the market place. There are many fine timber-framed buildings with handsome plasterwork and projecting storeys, not least of which are the Kings Head and Crown Inn

BILDESTON -- NAUGHTON

1 Turn right along the main road then left down a lane before the Post Office onto the footpath parallel with a stream. At the junction of paths in sight of houses turn right going over the stile to continue parallel to the stream. Before the next stile turn right down hill over the stream by footbridge. Over the stile and cross the field on a well-maintained path.

2 Turn left along the road. After Great Copt Hall turn right over the footbridge. Follow the field-edge path to the stream in the valley. Turn left beside it to a footbridge by an ash. Over the stream to follow the field-edge path uphill the lane.

3 Turn left on the lane past Apple Tree Cottage. Turn right over a stile, cross a paddock next to a fence, then cross another stile. Continue to the hedge-end and cross the field into the vale.

4 At the deep ditch turn left to the very wide earth bridge turning right over this uphill beside the stream. Turn left to walk the right side of the hedge. In the corner of the field at crosspaths turn right. Follow a ditch uphill to a corner and go through a gap in the hedge.

5 In the field turn left and walk to the right of a hedge. At the slight kink in the hedge by the young oak pass through the hedge to walk with it to your left. *You may see Naughton church tower among the trees ahead.* In the corner of the field cross the footbridge and walk diagonally across the meadow. Ignore the footbridge opposite instead walk along the thatched house boundary fence and over the sleeper steps and stile to the village green Naughton.

NAUGHTON -- LANGHAM CLOSE WOOD

3km / **2 miles** (Total 63km / 39.5ml) **Map 196** (155 / 1030)

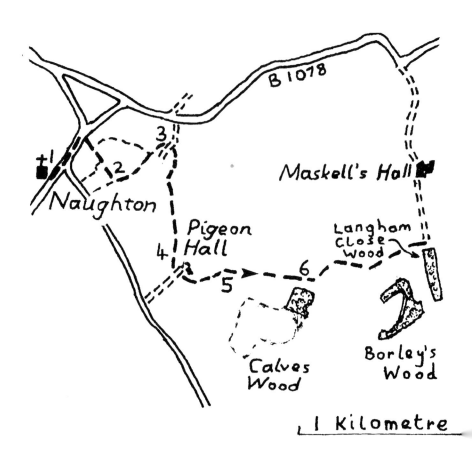

NAUGHTON -- LANGHAM CLOSE WOOD

1 Walk to the road. Turn left passing The Wheelhouse pub. Turn right before the pond on a track to a field. Move to the right and follow the line of poplars on the field edge. Continue to the field corner. Go over the twin-sleeper bridge.

2 Left along the side of the ditch/hedge towards the large farm building. Over the wide earth bridge in the corner. Continue into the next field along the same ditch towards Brickhouse Farm. Over the earth bridge in the corner. Walk the field edge tending left round the large farm building and farmhouse. Now walk beside the clipped hedge in the field parallel to the drive.

3 At the wide gap go onto the drive and walk back on yourself a short way . Now turn left to the far corner of a small triangular grass field.. Go round the left edge of the next field beside a ditch. Come to a grass track. Continue round the next field on this up a slope into a large field by an ash pollard. Walk the same track beside the sinuous hedge rounding the corner.

4 Cross footbridge into adjacent field. Cross field to left of Pigeon Hall Farmhouse. Cross farmyard. Buildings to the left of you, buildings to the right of you, out into the field with the pond on your left. Cross the field to the grassy field-edge track and cross the earth bridge on your left into the next field.

5 Turn right with the hedge to your right walk to cross a twin-sleeper bridge over a ditch. Walk beside a ditch to the corner of the field below what remains of Calves Wood
Calves Wood *was a nine hectare ancient wood. Eight hectares were cleared leaving a one hectare square.*

6 Turn left along a grassy track beside a ditch and hedge. When in sight of Borley's Wood and Langham Close Wood, cross the very wide earth bridge and turn left to walk on the right of a ditch to the left end of Langham Close Wood.

LANGHAM CLOSE WOOD -- OFFTON

2.5km / **1.5 miles** (Total 65.5km/41ml) **Map 196** (155/1030)

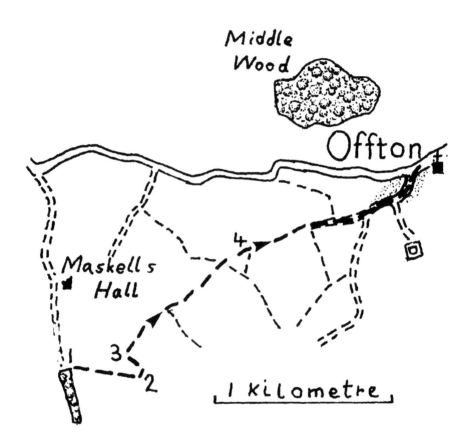

LANGHAM CLOSE WOOD -- OFFTON

Borley's Wood *is a strangely shaped three hectare ancient wood with oak standards, and ash-maple-hazel coppice.*

Langham Close Wood *is half the size of Borley's Wood. Long and narrow, it is all that remains of a much larger ancient wood*

1 Cross the farm drive to walk to the right of the field drainage ditch. After about 100m transfer to the left side of the ditch.

2 In the corner of the field turn left by the single ash tree to the next corner. Turn left again then right over the ditch with the ditch to your right.

3 Continue on the left side downhill over a ditch by twin-sleeper bridge tending to the right. Walk into the narrow end of a field.

4 Go over the wide earth bridge and walk to the left of a ditch/hedge. At the corner of the field, with the pylon visible, walk down between the two hedges onto the track towards houses. The tarmac lane takes you to a road junction in Offton.

OFFTON -- SOMERSHAM

2.5km / **1.5 miles** (Total 68km / 42.5ml) **Map 196** (155 / 1030)

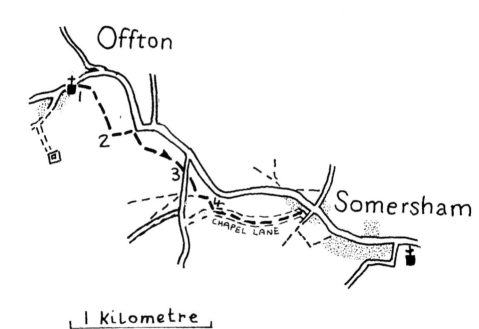

1 Kilometre

OFFTON -- SOMERSHAM

1 Turn right along the edge of the road to the far side of the open churchyard passing St.Marys Church on the eastern edge of the village. Cross over the road to the wide footbridge.

Look down at the **stream bank**. *You can see the chalk that underlies the boulder clay. Now look up across the field. You can see magnificent ancient* **Middle Wood** *above the village.*

Cross the road and leave it steeply uphill diagonally across the field to the outside corner of two hedges. Follow the hedge along the valley side crossing the farm track. Continue on the same course to the concrete track.

2 Turn left down the track to the bridge Turn right before the bridge to walk beside the stream. Go through the hedge gap and twin-sleeper bridge. Follow the hedge for about 100m until it veers to the left. At which point continue straight on across the field parallel with the hedge to the lane.

3 Cross the lane and the field ahead on the same course as before. Aim for the lone fir tree in the field. Pass to the right of a footbridge on to the green lane called Chapel Lane.

4 Turn left and walk down the lane to Somersham and the Duke of Marlborough.

SOMERSHAM -- BAYLHAM

5km/**3miles** (Total73km/45.5ml)**Maps196&211**(155/1030,1007)

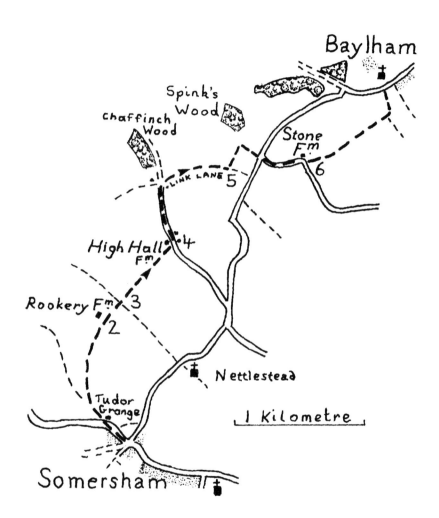

SOMERSHAM -- BAYLHAM

1 Turn left down the road over the bridge. Turn the corner left past the half-timbered house and turn right into the farmyard having the notice " Blakenham Farms Watering Farm Nettlestead ". Take the first left before the black weatherboarded out-building along the track.

2   Where the track enters Rookery Farm continue straight on along the field-edge path downhill. Over the stile then half right across the corner of the field through the gateway into the next field.

3 Turn left crossing the field to the stile and footbridge. Follow the field-edge path ahead passing right into the next field to past appropriately named High Hall onto a lane.

4 Turn left along the lane. At the left bend turn right along the grassy byway (Link Lane).

*Behind you over to the left is the east boundary of ancient **Chaffinch Wood** with its rare double medieval boundary bank of unknown function..* Go under the pylon to the path junction.

5 Turn left to the pylon in the field. Pass it and after a further 100m turn right on the grass strip.

*There is a lovely view of **Baylham Church** with ancient **Spink's Wood** near you to the left. Spink's Wood is all of 2.6ha with a woodline of ash standards and a hazel understorey. The northern half is dominated by young elm.*
Walk onto the sunken path and out to the road junction. Go straight over along the lane to Stone Farm.

6 At the bend in the lane keep straight along a track beside a hedge changing from left to the right some way along. Go under the pylon and follow the track down to the road at Baylham.

BAYLHAM -- CODDENHAM

5.5k / **3.5 miles** (Total78.5km/49ml)**Maps 211** (155,156/1007)

1 Turn right on the road and immediately left to walk up Church Lane passing St.Peters church and Glebe Close.

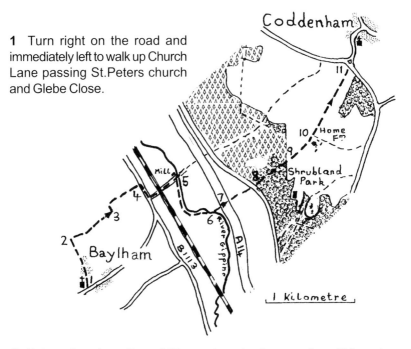

St.Peters churchyard is a wildlife sanctuary having more than 40 flowering species including rare Suffolk flowers such as fairy flax and meadow saxifrage..
Go along the entrance drive to just past Glebe Cottage. Veer right on a path at the cottage vegetable patch. Go round a barrier. Cross the pasture to another barrier. Walk on the left of the hedge to the end.
2 Turn right and follow the track downhill.
3 On the far side of the hedge coming in from the left, turn left along a footpath along the top of the horse paddock. At the end of the paddock turn right walking downhill past other paddocks. Leave through a wire door to the B1113.
4 Cross the road. Turn right along the pavement. Left along Mill Lane over the railway to the disused watermill by the River Gipping.

48

5 Turn right before the bridge over a stile. Walk beside of the river. Cross footbridge and along the riverbank to Sharmford Bridge

6 Over the river on this footbridge, turning right to the A14.

Sharmford Mere is the water-filled gravel pit to your left stocked with brown and rainbow trout and course fish. A survey of this wildlife site undertaken in 1992 revealed its great value for birdlife and plants and also 21 butterfly species, 8 dragonfly species, four reptile and amphibian species and 8 mammal species.

7 CROSS THE MAIN ROAD WITH EXTREME CAUTION

8 On the far side go over the stile across the meadow and over the Norwich Road. *At the entrance to Shrubland Park is a notice "Please do not disturb the breeding adders".* Go up the drive. Look for deer in the enclosure on your right..

Shrubland Park is on English Heritage's Register of Parks and Gardens of Special Historic Interest. The house is an eighteenth century Italianate Villa which is now a well known Health Club set in about 25 hectares of elaborate Italianate terraced gardens and grounds. You walk through the surrounding 175 ha. Park .

9 Leave drive at the five-bar gate going half-left on a grass path to walk beneath fine Spanish Chestnut trees. At the top of the slope cross level grass to a drive. Cross this over grass to the left of twin telegraph poles to a stile to the left of Home Farm.

10 After the stile go over the drive and another stile.Cross the corner of the field over another stile under the hawthorn.. Turn left through double metal gates and on beside the wire fence. Over a stile to walk along a track which opens into a large field.. The path is accompanied by a line of telegraph poles to the road.

11 Walk on the roadside over the bridge, then the pavement uphill. *To your left are* **Manor Farm Meadows** *four low-lying unimproved wet meadows registered as a County Wildlife Site.*

Turn left through

Coddenham churchyard *another fine example of unimproved meadowland being managed as a sanctuary for wildlife.*

CODDENHAM -- HEMINGSTONE PARISH

3km / **2 miles** (Total 81.5km / 51ml) **Map 211** (156 / 1007)

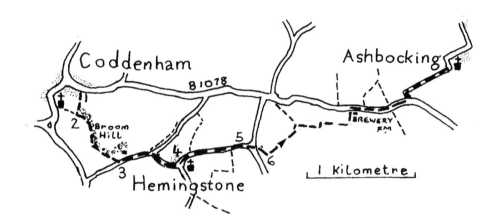

CODDENHAM -- HEMINGSTONE PARISH

1 Opposite the Dukes Head Pub, at the end of a terrace of houses, turn right uphill to Broom Hill. A notice reads:

BROOM HILL Bought by the people of Coddenham with help from the Countryside Commission, to be a natural area for all to enjoy. Looked after by the village with support from the Suffolk Wildlife Trust. March 1988.

2 Turn left to walk through Broom Hill wood tending downhill out onto a drive and hence to a lane.

3 Turn left to pass Hemingstone Hall and at the junction with Rectory Road turn right going steeply up Barham Road. At the top of the hill opposite St.Gregory Church.

4 Turn left on the Ashbocking Road (Church Lane). *To your left Just before the junction, if you were in a hot-air balloon, you would possibly see the square enclosure cropmark that suggests it may have at one time been a moat.*

5 At the Hemingstone junction cross over. Just to the right of the brick entrance to " Hillcrest " walk the public footpath beside a hedge to the corner. Cross a sleeper bridge into a back garden. Turn left immediately and cross another sleeper-bridge to the corner of an arable field.

6 Walk the field-edge path into the valley to the bottom hedge. Turn right and walk beside the hedge. Turn left near the end of the hedge to cross a narrow field, a concrete bridge and up a hedged track to the B1078. Turn right along this and cross the road to the start of the footpath opposite the house past Brewery Farm.

HEMINGSTONE -- HELMINGHAM

7km / **4.5 miles** (Total 88.5km/55.5ml) **Map 211** (156 / 1007)

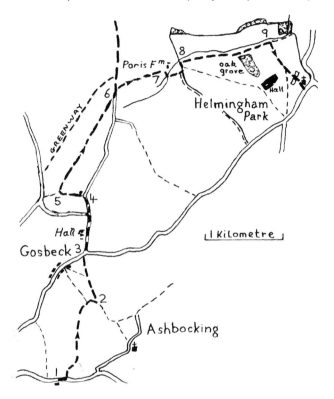

1 Follow field edge path for somewhile. Just past the corner a path leaves over sleepers to your left. Ignore this and instead continue on the field-edge permitted path onto a driveway.

2 Left down the drive to the lane on the outskirts of Gosbeck.

3 Go right to the junction, then left up the lane. Where the lane turns left instead continue straight on up the lane ahead. Go to the right bend before Elm Farm..

4 Turn left along the footpath. Go along the field-edge path next to the screen of Lawrence Cypress. As the path bends left turn right to cross the twin-sleeper bridge.

52

5 Cross the grass into the corner. The pig farm is to your right.
Through the opening on the left. Immediately turn right over the cross-field path to the outward corner. Continue in the same direction on the left of the ditch to the corner by a small pond. Cross the sleeper.
*Do you sense the airiness and elevation of this area of Suffolk? You have walked enough of this part of the county to appreciate why the inhabitants call it **High Suffolk***.
Field-edge paths eventually lead you out onto Pettaugh Lane.
6 Go left and walk the concrete drive to Paris Farm
7 Before entering the farmyard turn right beside the hedge. Cross the stream and veer left over the pasture on a grass track to the outside of Helmingham park. Turn left to the step-ladder stile. Over this into the park.
***Helmingham Park** is a 162ha deer park formed in the mid-sixteenth century. It is owned by the Tollemache family through trustees as is the rest of the parish.*
8 Walk straight out across the park to a bridge over the stream.
Over to your right is an**obelisk** on a mound. *The mound was a wilderness garden surrounded by a brick wall. The wall bricks were used in 1860 to build the obelisk.* Carry on along the grass path to the right of the stream. *You will probably see the herds of **Fallow and Red Deer***.
The open wood to your right is **Oak Grove** *a four hectare ancient wood heavily grazed by the deer.*
9 At the brick and flint bridge turn right going towards the Hall. Over the post and rail fence into the paddock. *Many of the **oaks** in the park started life in the 13th. and 14th..centuries, the two wonderful trees here are probably older.* Out the timber gate and the high metal gate beyond. Follow the drive round the pond. ***Helmingham Hall** is fifteenth century with later additions.* Cross the lawn and the causeway between *two rectangular* **fishponds** to **St.Marys Church**.*The church with its Tollemache memorials is worth a visit. Back outside look up at the tower crenellation the Tollemache crest gets*

HELMINGHAM -- KITTLE'S CORNER

6.5 km/**4 miles**(Total 95 km/59.5ml)**Map 211**(156/1007,1008)

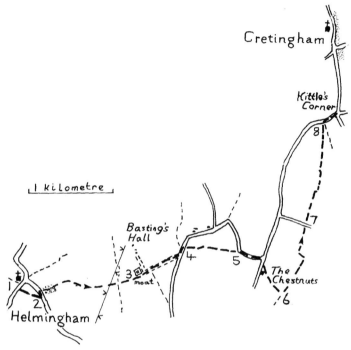

1 Cross the road opposite the church going over the field, a footbridge, and the next field to the corner and the lane

2 Left a short way to the metal gate on right. Through this and remnant small wood. Over stream by concrete bridge heading uphill on the right of the hedge to the corner. Go through the gap in the hedge continuing in the same direction beside the hedge beyond. In the corner go through adjoining hedge on earth bridge . Stay on same course. Under the cables, then over the earth bridge at the next hedge and on to the moat.

Basting's Hall moat*. The square water-filled moat surrounds the medieval site of Basting's Hall. It is covered by a deciduous wood, the new Hall having relocated 200m north.*

54

HELMINGHAM -- KITTLE'S CORNER

3 Keep straight on down the tarmac drive to the lane. Turn left along it for about 50m.

4 After a wide gap in the hedge on your right, pass through the laneside hedge into the paddock. Walk across this beside the hedge on your right. Through the timber five-bar gate then across the rough pasture tending to the left of centre. Through the broken gate into the field. Cross the field to the far right-hand corner. Over the sleeper. Walk to the right of the field ahead. Go over an earth bridge in the corner and then walk to the lane.

5 Continue in the same direction down the lane to a junction. Right on the Otley Road. Soon, on the left, at signs of habitation, go over sleeper-bridge walking to the left of hedge, then right, over sleeper-bridge through hedge. Walk over rough grassland to gateposts 25m left of large oak. Over another rough pasture tending left to far corner. Through wide gap walking left side of hedge ahead to corner. Through gap and cross narrow field to cross footbridge.

6 Turn left to walk beside the hedge then grass track down middle of narrow rough ground. Just past the old brick stable turn left onto drive. Walk this round Shrubbery Farmhouse to lane.

7 Straight over and along footpath, over twin-sleeper bridge, continue to follow field-edge path at corner cross sleeper-bridge. Cross narrow field to left of hedge. In corner turn right over ditch on a long twin-sleeper bridge. Turn left, walk beside ditch and hedge, through old metal gate. Go across paddock through another gate onto lane.

8 Turn right and walk to junction at Kittle's Corner.

KITTLE'S CORNER -- BRANDESTON

3 km / **2 miles** (Total 98 km / 61.5 ml) **Map 212** (156/1008,986)

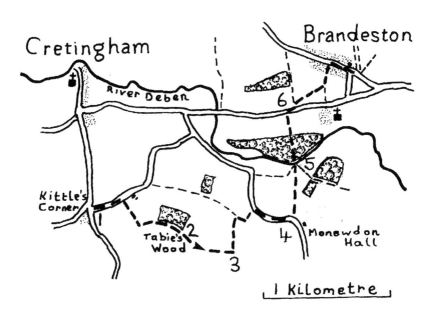

1 Take the Brandeston Road towards Poplar Farm.

Over to your right down the slope are a row of three small fields called
"The Spong" *enclosed by broad high hedgerows the meadows are host*
to many common flowering plants as well as the more rare bee orchid
and adder's tongue fern.
Where the hedge adjoins the road from the left, turn right (by the footpath
sign) to walk straight across the field, towards the church tower, to the
valley hedge. Over an earth bridge. Turn left beside stream, over the
twin-sleeper bridge to Tabie's Wood.

56

KITTLE'S CORNER -- BRANDESTON

Tabie's Wood *This three hectare ancient coppice-wood in Monewden parish has Cretingham parish boundary on the north and west edges and Brandeston parish boundary on the east edge.*

Walk past the wood beside the stream.

2 Continue beside the stream over an earth bridge in the field corner. *View Monewden Church to your right.* .Continue by the stream to the corner.

3 Turn left over a brick and concrete earth-topped bridge. Head uphill across the small field. Go through the hedge gap and over the ditch to walk uphill with a hedge on your right to Chestnut Tree Farm. Walk down the drive to the lane and turn right.

4 At the right-hand bend before Monewden Hall, turn left along the field-edge path. Go over a pole stile then walk down across the meadow. Over another pole stile to cross the River Deben by footbridge.

5 Walk along the path through the wood over two more footbridges. Walk beside the line of mature oaks to the left of the playing fields to the road and turn right.

6 At a hedge on your left, cross the stile and across a pasture tending right parallel with telegraph poles. Go through a kissing gate, over a three-sleeper bridge and walk to the left of the football pitch to the road. You are in the village of Brandesdon.

BRANDESTON -- FRAMLINGHAM

5km / **3 miles** (Total 103km / 64.5ml) **Map 212** (156 / 986)

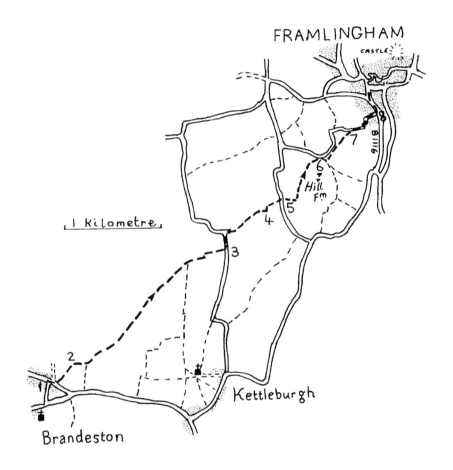

1 Turn right passing on your left, the Queen's Head Pub and Mutton lane, on the corner of which, opposite "The Broadhurst", go through the metal field gate on the grass track public footpath. Over the pasture and to the right of the pond leave the track tending left going over the corner metal gate.

BRANDESTON -- FRAMLINGHAM

2   Walk to the right of the ditch ahead to the corner. Over the stream onto the track. Turn half-left to cut off the corner of the field back to the track. Follow this going over the earth bridge in the corner. Continue to walk beside the stream but this time with it on your right. At the corner ignore the wide earth bridge ahead, instead turn left about fifteen metres to stay on the track. Turn left at the next earth bridge to skirt a pond on a field-edge path. Walk to the corner and through gap in hedge over the twin-sleeper bridge. Cross twin-sleeper bridge over stream, over the track, follow the left side of the hedge. Cross an earth bridge through a pocket of elm and thorn scrub now walking to the right of the stream. Take the field-edge path to the right of the hedge ahead. Up over the rise and turn left under the cables then left to continue beside the ditch. Walk round the field-edge path then over an earth bridge onto the lane

3 Left to the two cottages before which turn right through the wood over the twin-sleeper bridge out into a field. Follow beside the ditch towards Framlingham church seen in the distance. At the corner of the field with a ditch in front of you, about fifty metres from the farm buildings, move to the left of the ditch.

4 Through hedge after corner onto concrete pad Walk between the hedge and the chicken shed of Lampards Farm to the lane.

5   Cross, Take field-edge path left of hedge. Turn corner left to next corner. Right to Ashing Grove Turn left over a concrete bridge and walk beside wood. Tend left round outbuildings then through Hill Farm yard. Left down drive to before lane.

6 Right over stile to cross paddock beside the hedge. Over the next stile to continue beside the hedge. Go through the gap in the hedge in front of you over the twin-sleeper bridge. Aiming for the church tower, cross the arable field onto the lane.

7 Turn right down the lane to B 1116 by Station Hotel.

8 Turn left to the town, turning right up Albert Place/Fore street at the junction. Now turn left opposite St.Clares Catholic Church down a cul-de-sac, up a path, through a covered walkway out into Framlingham market square.

FRAMLINGHAM -- SAXTEAD GREEN

4km / **2.5 miles** (Total 107km / 67ml) **Map 212** (156 / 986)

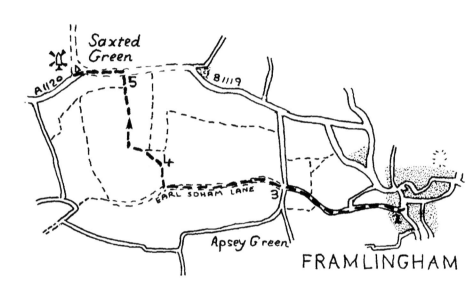

Saxted Green

A1120

B1119

15

4

EARL SOHAM LANE   3

Apsey Green

FRAMLINGHAM

1 Kilometre

FRAMLINGHAM -- SAXTEAD GREEN

Framlingham developed round the market place with the church and castle nearby. Lovely shop fronts along Castle Street. Double Street got its name because it was the first street in Fram. To have houses and shops either side. It has an early Victorian pillar-box. Would you say the parish **Church of St.Michael** *has one of the most beautiful church roofs in Suffolk? The twelfth century* **castle** *is a fine early example of a fortified curtain wall castle with thirteen towers. To the west is* **Framlingham Mere**, *its sedge marsh and open water of the mere provide good conditions for overwintering birds such as gadwall, jack snipe, shoveler and wigeon with breeding birds in abundance such as lesser whitethroat, marsh tit, reed bunting, sedge warbler, spotted flycatcher and treecreeper.*

1 Retrace your steps going back through the arch down to Fore Street / Albert Place. Turn right to the junction then left along Station Road.

2 Opposite the Funeral Directors and Builders turn right to walk up Brook Lane. This narrows as the lane becomes country. Continue to the left bend where you turn right over the brook and immediately turn left along green Earl Soham Lane.

3 Walk this green lane to the field. Continue beside the hedge to the corner of the large field. Turn right on the bridleway beside ditch and hedge. At the corner cross the wide sleeper bridge into the field a short way then turn half-left to a small open area with young trees. Layen's Barn used to stand here.

4 Walk over to your left towards the left end of a long hedge. A short distance before the hedge turn right to cut across the corner of the field. At the track beside the hedge continue to eventually come out onto the B 1119.

5 Turn left through Saxtead Green to the windmill.

SAXTEAD GREEN -- TANNINGTON

5km / **3 miles** (Total 112km / 70ml) **Map 212** (156 / 986)

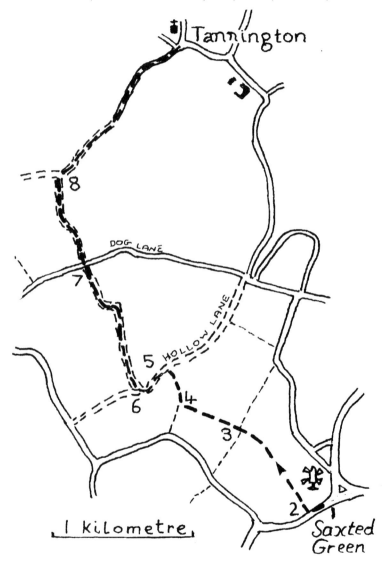

SAXTEAD GREEN -- TANNINGTON

*The **Post Mill** on Saxtead Green is one of the finest in England. It was a working mill from 1796 to 1947. There have been windmills in the parish and probably on this site since before 1309. The buck (body) of the mill revolves round the central millpost with the sails kept facing the wind by the fantail.*

*The **unimproved grassland** north of the mill and this side of the A1120 contains various lovely plant species including agrimony, ox-eye daisy and pepper saxifrage and the two long thin ponds, plants such as false fox sedge, gypsywort and reedmace.*

1 Take the main Earl Soham road and just past the toilets and road sign turn right on the field-edge path.

2 Walk on to the cross-field path and on over the stile, the grass field verge then the next stile. You now walk on the right of the ditch

3 Continue beside the ditch to the corner going over the earth bridge and the arable field beyond.

4 At the bridleway junction turn right to Hollow Lane.

5 Turn left along this green lane to the junction of paths.

6 Turn right along Bullswood Lane. The signpost says to Bedfield and Tannington.

7 Cross Dog Lane and continue north on the green lane

As you pass through the double bend look at the trees. There are some hornbeam including a pollard.

8 At the junction with the track turn right along it going through a *tiny triangular wood that contains hornbeam as well as elm trees.* Continue to Tannington and the church.

TANNINGTON -- BRUNDISH

5.5km / **3.5 miles** (Total 117.5km/73.5ml)**Map 230** (156/ 986)

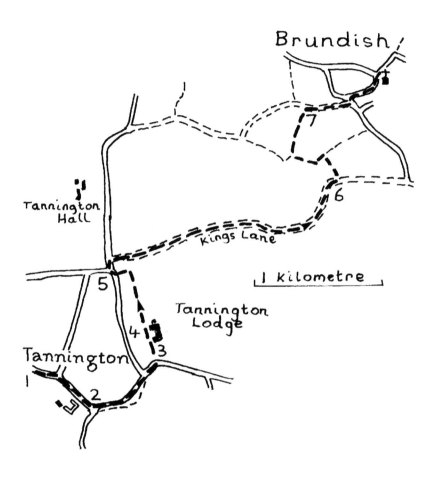

Tannington *has six medieval moated sites within the parish and three big old houses - Tannington Place, Tannington Hall and Braiseworth Hall. By way of contrast much of the parish ancient field pattern with its lacework of hedges has been grubbed out.*

TANNINGTON -- BRUNDISH

1 Right, down the road to junction. Right past Braiseworth Hall.

2 At the junction turn left and at the next junction continue straight on to the right - hand bend.

3 Turn left through the shrubs over the sleeper bridge and stile into the long narrow rough meadow. Walk to the right near a hedge with a wide still stream. *This becomes the impressive medieval moat adjacent to Tannington Lodge.*

4 Pass the lodge over the drive and a track to the arable field. Go in the same direction along the field edge to the far corner where you must pass through the hedge and turn left to cross the field to the cottage by the road.

5 Right to junction. Right for about fifty metres to concrete King's Lane. Follow bridleway beyond muck pile where the lane becomes earth. Continue, turning a right bend past two fine oaks. Stop between hedges about 100 metres after the bend.

6 Turn left through the hedge over the ditch into the large arable field. *Hedgerows would have guided you over the next part of your way but unfortunately a farmer has grubbed them out and the underlying possibly medieval **field system** and **trackway** have been ploughed out.* Head out across the field tending a little left for about 175m to the pond. Walk round this to the left then strike out into the field SW (towards the giant muck heap) for about 50m. Now turn and walk 1000m WNW into the large field. (Having Fun!) Lastly turn northwards and head down the slope to the trees.

7 In a corner by the ivy-clad pollard, cross onto the green lane by sleeper bridge. Turn right along the lane onto the tarmac lane in Brundish. Cross over and walk up the lane, with the young River Alde (no more than a stream) to your right, to the church.

BRUNDISH -- LAXFIELD

5.5km/**3.5miles**(Total123km/77ml)**Maps230&231**(156/986,965)

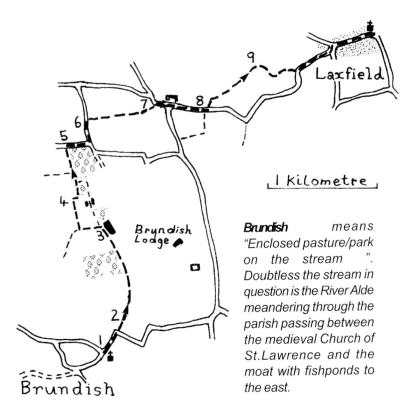

Brundish means "Enclosed pasture/park on the stream ". Doubtless the stream in question is the River Alde meandering through the parish passing between the medieval Church of St.Lawrence and the moat with fishponds to the east.

1 Continue along the lane to corner. Pass through a field gate, a stock enclosure, then another gate. Walk the length of the long ,narrow pasture and cross into the arable field over the earth bridge in the right corner.

2 Follow the line of telegraph poles across the arable field to the left corner by the pond. Turn the pond on the left to walk along the edge of an orchard to the left of a ditch/hedge. This takes you onto a track leading to the left of a reservoir

3 Half-way along the reservoir turn left beside the orchard with a deep ditch to your left. At the concrete bridge turn right along the next side of this orchard at first to the left of shelter alders then,after about 50m, at the thorn hedge pass through into a field to walk on the left side to the corner. Now turn right following the hedge to the next corner, passing a pond on your right.

4 Walk the field-edge path to the lane.

5 Turn right along the lane and at the junction turn left on the Wilby/ Stradbrooke road.

6 After Lane Farm, but before the slight bend to the left, turn right to cross the arable field to the corner of a distant hedge (not the nearest hedge that is to your left). Cross the ditch and walk on the left of the hedge to Stirrup Street.

7 Turn right along the "street" to the junction. *Elms Farm is surrounded by the remaining parts of a medieval moat. View of Laxfield Church to your left..* Keep straight on at the junction along the Laxfield/Halesworth Road.

8 A little before the isolated oak, that is on the right side of the road, turn left over the ditch to cross the corner of the arable field to the corner of a ditch 60m or so away. Turn this round to the left and walk with the ditch to your right on the field edge. Over the earth bridge and continue.

9 In the corner cross the field beside the Xmas trees to the hedge. Now turn right until about 50m before the pylon and bear left to continue to follow the hedge. Near the corner turn left over the sleeper bridge. Cross the arable field to the hedge. Turn right on the headland path to the lane. Turn left along it and at the junction turn right through Laxfield.

LAXFIELD -- UBBESTON

3km / **2 miles** (Total 126km / 79ml) **Map 231** (156 / 965)

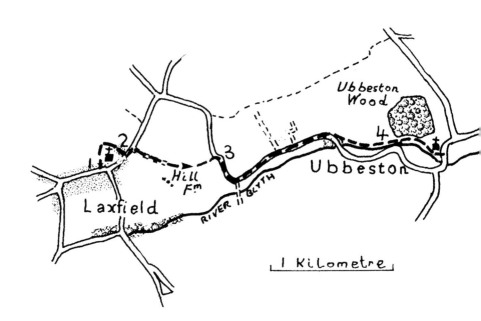

LAXFIELD -- UBBESTON

Laxfield has special appeal. The broad main street,, sad empty shops, the church, the splendid former Guildhall on the corner, the Low House.

1 Opposite the *Guildhall*, turn left at the corner of the churchyard down Church Villas pathway then right down Church Walk. Pass the *Low House pub*. Turn left up the lane.

2 Opposite Blyth House turn right along the tarmac cul-de-sac. Through the hedge to your right. ***Laxfield Meadows****. These two unimproved grassland fields contain species of flowering plant such as cowslip, ox-eye daisy, pepper saxifrage and quaking grass. There is also plentiful rare adder's-tongue fern. These two meadows are part of only three percent species-rich meadows to have survived farmers since the second world war in Suffolk.*

Pass Hill Farm on grass track to end of hedge. Turn right to the corner and walk the field-edge permissive path down to house, turning the corner to cross a sleeper bridge onto the lane.

3 Turn right and follow this delightful lane to the five-bar timber gate at the right-hand bend before the hump-backed bridge. Turn half-left through the gate to cross the willow plantation then over the stile. Walk beside the River Blyth to the bend then continue in the same direction passing close to an apple tree to the wood edge.

4 This really is a magical place. Walk beside the river through the edge of ancient Ubbeston Wood.
Ubbeston Wood *slopes up on your left covering 9.5 hectares. It is predominantly hornbeam but there are areas of ash, hazel and maple on ill-drained soil. A rare plant for Suffolk is found along the rides which is indicative of ancient woodland, it is the thin-spiked wood sedge.* Come out onto a lawn. Cross by the hedge onto the drive and hence to the lane below the church.

UBBESTON -- HUNTINGFIELD

4km / **2.5 miles** (Total 130km / 81.5ml) **Map 231** (156 / 965)

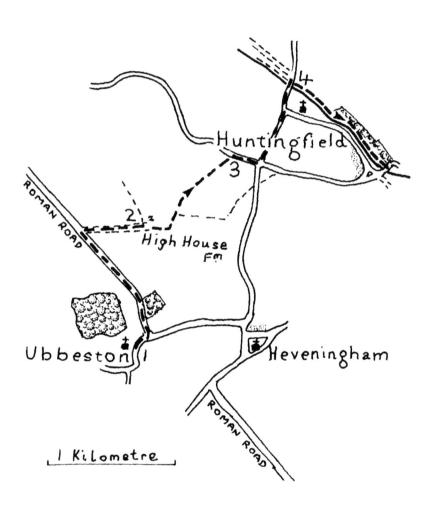

UBBESTON -- HUNTINGFIELD

1 At St.Peters church turn left along the lane to the junction. Turn left uphill on the Cratfield/Fressingfield Lane. This soon straightens to become a Roman Road. Turn right down High House Farm drive.

2 Leave the drive opposite the house to keep straight on along a grassy field-edge track. At the corner don't cross the ditch, instead, turn left on the grassy track round the hornbeam pollard. Follow this coming out at Brian Woods Garage on the lane.

3 Turn right and at the crossroads turn left on the Huntingfield Church/ Linstead road. *View of Heveningham Hall to your right.* Pass the church turn off. Go over the white post and pipe bridge.

4 Turn right along the field-edge path . Pass the grand old pollarded hornbeam over the stile and into the wood. Walk the raised track coming out on a lane in Huntingfield.

HUNTINGFIELD -- CHEDISTON

5.5km / **3.5 miles** (136km / 85ml) **Map 231** (156 / 965)

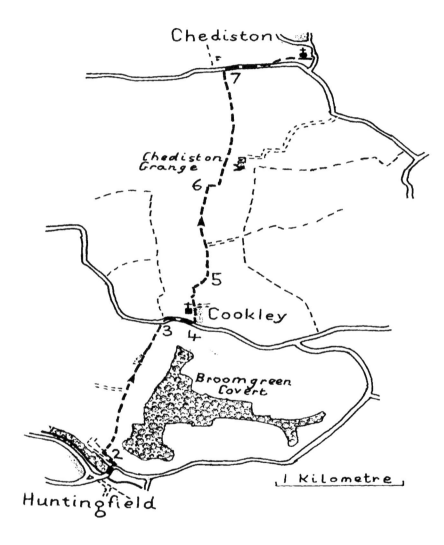

HUNTINGFIELD -- CHEDISTON

There is a pub on the green.

1 Turn right along Bridge Street to the corner of the wood. Turn left on the public footpath to Cookley beginning as Huntington Hall driveway.

2 Before the cattlegrid turn right along the field-edge path tending left. Through the hedge gap over the twin-sleeper bridge. Keep on this course uphill beside the hedge. Near the top go on the concrete track all the way to Cookley. *Lovely view of Cookley.*

3 The next part of the route may have been officially diverted, therefore, follow the diversion, but at the time of writing the right of way is as follows. Turn right and walk past the church.

4 Turn left along the sandy drive passing the church out to a field. Stride out across the arable field 100m uphill to the left edge of the clump of trees. Continue in the same direction to the right hand end of a hedge by the crabapple tree.

5 Cross the shallow ditch to the corner of a field and walk ahead to the left of the hedge. At the corner pass through the hedge and turn right crossing the ditch to turn left walking the right side of the ditch.

6 Continue past the ditch coming in from your right to the corner. Turn right for about 50m then turn left over the grassy earth bridge to follow the track left of the hedge. Leave the track where it turns right to Chediston Grange to cross the field corner. Turn left along the grass track to its end. Continue in the same direction over the field to the footbridge and B1123.

7 Turn right along the road to about 100m before the bridge. Turn half-left over a stile across a paddock then another stile on to the white memorial cross in the churchyard in Chediston

CHEDISTON -- HALESWORTH

3km / **2 miles** (Total 139km/87ml)**Map 231** (156/965 or 966)

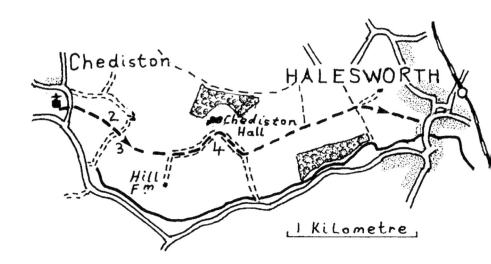

CHEDISTON -- HALESWORTH

1 Continue along the track parallel to the church to the lane. Cross over the lane and the twin-sleeper bridge. Walk across the field parallel to the wall on your right over rough ground. Keep to the left of the hedge going over the heavy stile and twin-sleeper bridge. Go uphill to the left of a hedge for about 50m and turn right over a stile.

2 Turn half-left to cross the small field uphill to a stile in the hedge. Clamber over the stile and cross the pasture to the right-hand corner. Go over the stile and across the ditch by a twin sleepers to enter a large field.

3 Walk across the field. There is a telegraph pole you walk to. From this follow the ditch to the hoggin farm track. Walk uphill along the track to go round the pond at Chediston Hall.

4 On to the tarmac track downhill. Turn left part way down the hill and walk the track to a bend by a small wood. Leave the track by continuing straight on over a stile, turning half-right, cross a pasture. Through the kissing gate, walk up School Lane to the junction. Turn right on Rectory Street and down into Halesworth.

HALESWORTH -- BLYFORD

4km / **2.5 miles** (Total 142.5km / 89.5ml) **Map 231** (156 / 966)

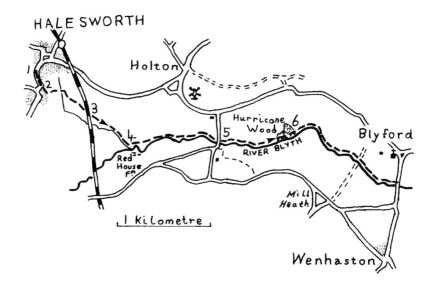

Halesworth has a compact town centre with a pleasant pedestrianised main shopping street and parish church at the southern end which has an area of land given in 1896 as an open space for the public. Apparently the water from mineral springs near Halesworth contain something that is able to heal inflamed eyes. River Blyth is the south boundary of the parish. Suffolk Way follows the course of the river to the sea.

1 Turn right along Bridge Street. At the end turn left, opposite Lloyds Bank, on the road that curves to the left round a carpark. Go to the opposite side of the roundabout down River Lane.

76

HALESWORTH -- BLYFORD

2 Walk across the concrete bridge and at the waterway turn right beside it. This is in fact a tributary of the Blyth called
New Reach River and the waters edge is a haven for gorgeous flowers such as ragged robin, yellow iris and water forget-me-not and also watercress. The water is home to plants such as broad-leaved pondweed, hornwort and starwort.
Through the gate then to a footbridge but do not go over it, instead continue round the edge of the field right After a 100 metres or so go over the stile, and pass under a railway bridge.

3 Walk across the footbridge to turn left beside a stream. Cross the footbridge turning right to continue walking beside the stream. You then cross a succession of footbridges and stiles until you face Red House Farm over the River Blyth.

4 The path turns left after the last footbridge to leave the river temporarily to cross a meadow to another footbridge. *View of **Holton Windmill** dated from 1749, ceased working in c.1900.* After which, walk along the left bank of the river over a succession of footbridges and stiles coming out onto a lane

5 Cross over down concrete path past " Holton Gauging Station " (Wooden Hut). Follow the left bank of the river and cross a stile by the crack willow. Cross the field keeping to the young River Blyth. Cross another stile by willows. Then in the corner go over another stile to walk through
***Hurricane Wood**, a poplar plantation with willow and alder along a meandering path through nettles. Trees were blown over in the October 1987 gale. Look out for otters.*

6 Cross the metal footbridge with a view of the water mill across the Blyth. Cross a succession of meadows interrupted by footbridges and stiles eventually coming out to Blyford Bridge with its *tidal barrier.*

BLYFORD — BLYTHBURGH

3km / **2 miles** (Total 146.5km / 91.5ml) **Map 231** (156 / 966)

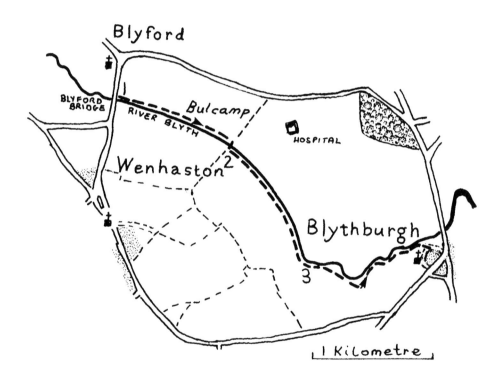

BLYFORD -- BLYTHBURGH

Blyford Bridge is a good vantage point to see the canalisation of the river a little to the west and down towards Blythburgh to the east which is tidal water.

1 Cross the road and walk the left bank of the Blyth over wet meadows crossing stiles to a reedbed. Walk along the river embankment through reeds to a concrete bridge below Bulchamp.

2 Cross the river going over a stile to walk the right bank of the river.

Blythburgh Hospital on the valleyside was constructed as Bulchamp Workhouse that opened in 1756, housing 46 paupers after being partly destroyed by a mob while under construction. It was converted to Blythburgh Hospital in the twentieth century.

Suddenly the **Church of the Holy Trinity, Blythburgh**, comes into view. No wonder it is known as the *"Cathedral of the Marches " at 128 feet long and 83 feet high it is an impressive landmark.*

3 Keep going towards the church but soon tend to the right through the reed marsh on a raised bank. It is not long before you are heading back in the direction of the church. Below the church on a little green beside the river turn right to walk up a footpath towards the church. Come out to the left of the church at Blythburgh. *Over to your northwest are* **Blythburgh Marshes** *that flood in the winter providing an excellent waterlogged feeding ground for wildfowl.*

BLYTHBURGH -- WALBERSWICK N.N.R.

2.5km / **1.5 miles** (Total 149km / 93ml) **Map 231** (156 / 966)

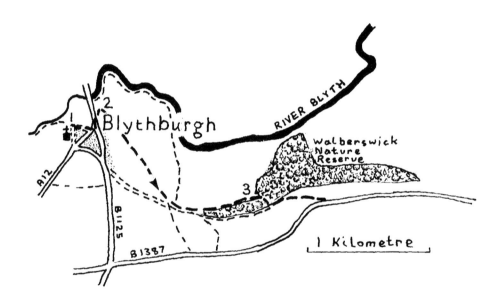

BLYTHBURGH -- WALBERSWICK N.N.R.

Blythburgh is a compact small village on the Blyth built to the east of the Church of the Holy Trinity and south of the river crossing. It was a prosperous port in the fifteenth century exporting wool but declined as the Blyth silted up. The church was built over an Augustine Priory, some of the remains of which are just NE of the church. Go in the church. The scorch marks on the door are ascribed to the devil. Admire the wood-pegged tie beam roof (no nails) and the roof angels. The bench ends depict the seven deadly sins

1 Walk straight down the lane to the B1125. Turn left, crossing the road to pass the White Hart Inn with its Dutch gables.
White Hart Inn was at one time a Quarter Sessions courthouse and retains much of its panelling and moulded ceiling beams.

2 Turn half-right down a dirt track. When the marshes come into view, take the footpath on your right going through a kissing gate into
Walberswick National Nature Reserve. The 514ha reserve was opened in 1972. The notice at the entrance tells us "This reserve was established to safeguard an outstanding mosaic of heathland, woods, marshes, mudflats, saltings and grazing marshes. It has a rich variety of birds and other wildlife, some of which are particularly sensitive to disturbance."
Angel Marshes to your left on the south side of the Blyth are part of the reserve, These inter-tidal mudflats and saltmarshs are important for wildfowl eg shelduck, and waders like dunlin, redshank, spotted redshank, and avocet.
Walk along the sea wall over a couple of footbridges and a stile to the sign " Horse riding only. No access on foot ".

3 Turn right along the footpath over the heath for about 45m then turn left on a wide track. Go along this out onto the B1187 at Tinker's Walks.

WALBERSWICK N.N.R -- WALBERSWICK

3km / **2 miles** (Total 152km / 95ml) **Map 231** (156 / 966)

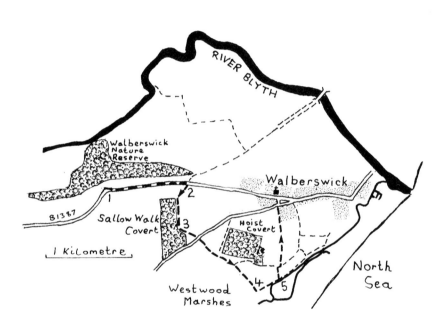

1 Walk south side of road towards Walberswick. ***Anti-glider ditches.***
Look each side as you walk and you should see a series of bracken-filled ditches. These are anti-glider defense ditches dug during the second world war to repel the Hun.

WALBERSWICK N.N.R. -- WALBERSWICK

2 When Walberswick church tower comes into view turn right on track. Right, after about 100m, on bridleway to Sallow Walk Covert. Turn left beside the wood with East Sheep Walk to your right. *From the middle ages into the twentieth century sheep grazed the heath here in spring and summer.*

3 Veer left on the track to Lodge Road. Over the road, down a track and turn left before a timber five-bar gate. Walk the track, with Hoist Covert to your left, onto Oldtown Marshes. *Hoist covert is predominately a birch and Scots pine wood planted in the early nineteenth century as cover for game.* Walk to the disused windpump tower. *You may be lucky and see the men cutting and stacking the reed for thatch.*

4 *Oldtown and Westwood Marshes Early in the eighteenth century the marshes were embanked, dykes dug and sluices installed and a brick windpump built to drain the marsh water into a canal and hence into the Dunwich River. This provided grazing marsh for cattle and horses. The coast here was seen as vulnerable to invasion so the grazing was flooded during the Second World War and once again it is a reedmarsh.*

It fact Westwood Marshes to the west are probably the largest freshwater reedbed in Britain attracting Marsh Harriers, Bitterns, bearded reedlings and water rail, to name but a few birds. With sensitive restoration and conversion, the windpump tower would make a fantastic bird hide.
Left over footbridge and walk beside the river for about 250m.

5 Turn left across the marsh and up the hillside to a rest on
" Mac's Seat ". Tend right of the seat on a grass track then the track between two fields towards the church tower. Come out onto the gravel lane, turn left to Lodge Road. Cross over and walk the gravel lane opposite. You come out at St.Andrews Church. Turn right to walk through Walberswick..

WALBERSWICK -- SOUTHWOLD

5km / **3 miles** (Total 157km / 98ml) **Map 231** (156 / 966)

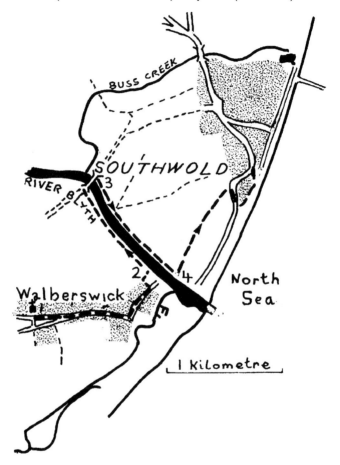

The **parish of Walberswick** is bounded north by the River Blyth (see previous map) and Westwood Marshes to the south. The village is spread beautifully along the B1389 seaward. You might be forgiven for assuming the North Sea forms the east boundary. In point of fact, only the beach at Town Salts is Walberswick, most of the shoreline is in the parishes of Dunwich or Southwold.

84

WALBERSWICK -- SOUTHWOLD

Walberswick was a large thriving medieval town but by the mid-sixteenth century it was in decline, any recovery not helped by it being prone to flooding and fires. One fire was before 1583 followed by three others in 1633, 1683 and 1749. In the last of these fires a third of the town was destroyed. As if that were not enough parishioners decided they could not afford to look after the large Church of St.Andrew so they were grant-aided to demolish it in 1695-96. The magnificent tower built in 1426 and southwest end remain among the ruins. Early in the twentieth century Walberswick was often the subject of the works of the artist Wilson Steer.

1 Walk down the street into Walberswick and down to the wonderful hodgepodge quay. Over to the right is **Walberswick Saltmarsh** *with its creeks important for invertebrates especially crabs. This is the only site in Suffolk where the plant Lesser Centaury is found..*

2 *G*ive the **ferry**man *your trade. The trip across the River Blyth by rowing boat is great fun.* If he is not there, turn left along the harbour riverbank on the sea defence to the footbridge.

3 Go over the bridge and turn right to walk the riverbank to the road opposite the ferry pier.

4 Take the path between **Town Marshes** and **Havenbeach Marshes.** *The marshes are a nationally importance habitat of grazing marsh, dykes and saltmarsh, providing food and cover for many species of bird including gadwall, shoveler, redshank, lapwing, snipe, short-eared owls and harriers. Havenbeach marshes to your right flood in winter which suits dunlin, ringed plover and whimbrel, among other species*.

Walk to the road below Gun Hill and hence into Southwold.

SOUTHWOLD -- EASTON BROAD

4km / **2.5 miles** (Total 161km / 100.5ml) **Map 231** (156 / 966)

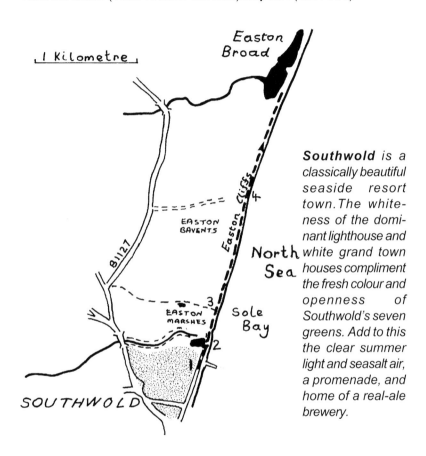

Southwold is a classically beautiful seaside resort town. The whiteness of the dominant lighthouse and white grand town houses compliment the fresh colour and openness of Southwold's seven greens. Add to this the clear summer light and seasalt air, a promenade, and home of a real-ale brewery.

The lighthouse is not as old as you might imagine. It was built in 1890 and is active at night throwing its beam from 100ft up 17 miles out to sea. Southwold parish is very nearly an island, with the Blyth to the south, Buss Creek to the west and north, and the sea to the east. It was a Saxon fishing port growing to a medieval town which declined as the harbour silted up.

86

SOUTHWOLD -- EASTON BROAD

1 From the promenade start the walk northwards along the coastline. You are about to enter an area with a complex combination of habitats giving splendidly prolific wildlife.

*Southwold boating lakes are an important are of open water for wintering wildfowl . West of the lakes are***Town Farm Marshes** *a Suffolk Wildlife Trust Reserve where you would see marsh and hen harriers and with luck the elusive grasshopper warbler.*

2 On up the coast of Sole Bay, ever closer to the end of your long walk from Flatford to Lowestoft, the seashore is the place to walk although the marshes inland are fascinating.

Sole Bay is so heavily eroded by the sea it is no longer a bay but retains the name. It was the scene of a navel battle in 1672 between the allies the English and French, against the Dutch.

Easton Marshes *where the shingle with dry sandy soil giving ground conditions appropriate for sticky groundsel, and the waterlogged marsh gives marsh and common spotted orchid..*
To the west of Easton Marshes **Bridge Foot Marshes** *are an ornithological paradise .*

3 Continue to walk along the beach unless you find it impassable due to high tides and stormy seas. If this is the case, you are advised to walk the coastland and the cliff top at Easton Cliffs.

Easton Cliffs *also known as* **Easton Bavents Cliffs** *after the parish in which they are found, these cliffs are composed of Wedleston Beds over Easton Bavents Clays over Norwich Crag (soft rock). The crag has yielded fossil bones of extinct species of horse, deer and elephant among other animals.*

4 Walk on to Easton Broad.

EASTON BROAD -- BENACRE BROAD

4km / **2.5 miles** (Total 165km/103ml) **Map 231** (156/966,946)

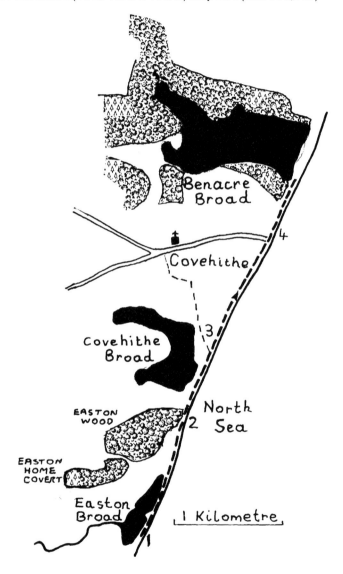

Benacre Broad

Covehithe

4

Covehithe Broad

3

EASTON WOOD

North Sea

2

EASTON HOME COVERT

Easton Broad

1 Kilometre

1

EASTON BROAD -- BENACRE BROAD

Easton Broad *Drainage dykes of the grazing marshes of Frostenden Valley supply fresh water flowing east becoming brackish in Easton Broad. This saltiness comes from seawater washed over the sand and shingle bar during stormy weather.*

1 Walk along the beach to Easton Wood.

Easton Wood *covers fifteen hectare. An internal valley consists of an alder glade. Around this are oak and sweet chestnut mature trees with a sweet chestnut understorey on dry sandy acid soil. This soil grows in the main a combination of bracken bramble and bluebells with a good population of climbing corydalis.*

2 Carry on up the coast to Covehithe Broad.

Covehithe Broad *is the second of the three shallow peat-bottomed ponds forming the southern outriders of the Suffolk Broads. The sand and shingle bar is quite noticeable and acts as a dam preventing the stream reaching the sea. The freshwater ponds-up to form Covehithe Broad. Shingle plants include Sea Pea, Yellow Horned-poppy and Sticky Groundsel.*
3 Walk on the beach if tides permit.

Covehithe Cliffs are a rich source of vertebrate fossils. If conditions are unfavourable take the clifftop path or you may wish to travel inland and visit the *seventeenth century* **church of St.Andrew** *built on the ruins of an early fourteenth century church.*

4 Go down to Benacre Broad.

BENACRE BROAD -- KESSINGLAND

3km / **2 miles** (Total 168km / 105ml) **Map 231** (156 / 946)

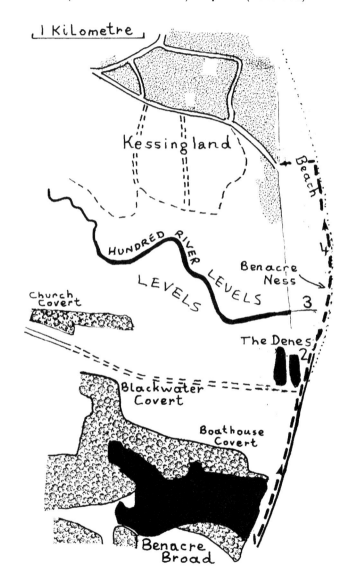

BENACRE BROAD -- KESSINGLAND

Benacre Broad *is the largest of the three broads with the northwest arm called the Bay of Biscay. It is fringed with extensive beds of the common reed and surrounded, apart from the seaward end, by self-sown alder, birch, sallow and oak. Outside of this are plantations of elm, Scots pine, sweet chestnut, and oak.Wildfowl floating on the broads include goldeneye, pochard, wigeon and tufted duck. In the air look out for Buzzards, Hen Harriers and Sparrowhawks*

1 Continue to walk along the beach to the Denes.
The Denes *are three water-filled old gravel pits.*

2 Walk to just beyond the Denes to the outflow of the Hundred River.
Kessingland Levels *are on either side of the river with its waterlilies and abundant darting dragonflies. The levels are an area of grazing marsh and true marsh, of considerable ornithological and botanical importance and are host to many species of wintering birds in great numbers, such as mallard, moorhen, mute swan, teal, wigeon and pochard.*

3 A short walk by the sea brings you onto Benacre Ness.
Benacre Ness *shingle headland with its relict dunes, (apart from Lowestoft Ness), is the most easterly place in England. It is definitely not a place to go for a swim. The strong tidal currents are moving Benacre Ness northwards (look at the direction of the breaking waves) whereas everywhere else along the east coast longshore drift is moving shingle southwards.*

4 Walk the shingle of Kessingland Beach by the sea.
Kessingland Beach *This delicate, harsh habitat is home to sea kale, sea pea and yellow-horned poppy. Shingle is being deposited onto the beach, which is in stark contrast to much of the East Coast which is being eroded.* Cross the shingle on the fishermen's mats into Kessingland.

KESSINGLAND -- PAKEFIELD

3km / **2 miles** (Total 171km / 107ml) **Map 231** (156 / 946)

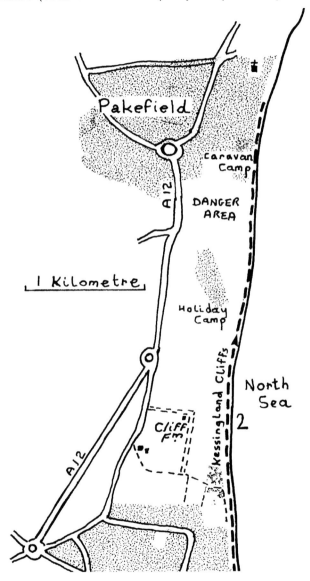

KESSINGLAND -- PAKEFIELD

Kessingland parish is dominated by extensive modern expansion of the village north of the B 1437 and holiday camps to the south accommodating thousands of holiday makers each year, and yet there is a sense of community in Kessingland.

1 Head north along the coastal footpath or beside the sea past Kessingland Cliffs.

Kessingland Cliffs The cliff scree slope is an interesting wildlife site with a colony of bee orchids and other uncommon plants such as bithynian vetch and biting stonecrop. Along the cliff-top there are areas of blackthorn and hawthorn scrub providing shelter for migrant songbirds

2 Walk on past Crazy Mary's Hole, and Pakefield Cliffs to Pakefield outside Lowestoft.

PAKEFIELD -- LOWESTOFT

3km/**2miles**(174km/109ml)**OutdoorLeisureMap40**(134 / 925)

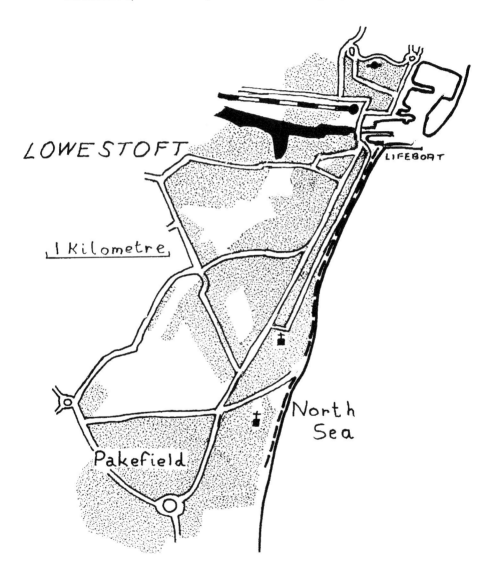

PAKEFIELD -- LOWESTOFT

Pakefield *is the southern most area of Lowestot, partly in the parish of Gisleham and partly in the borough of Lowestoft.*

Continue along the coast from Pakefield into Lowestoft.

The long walk is over at the Lifeboat Station at South Pier Lowestoft.

Well done. I hope you enjoyed your journey.